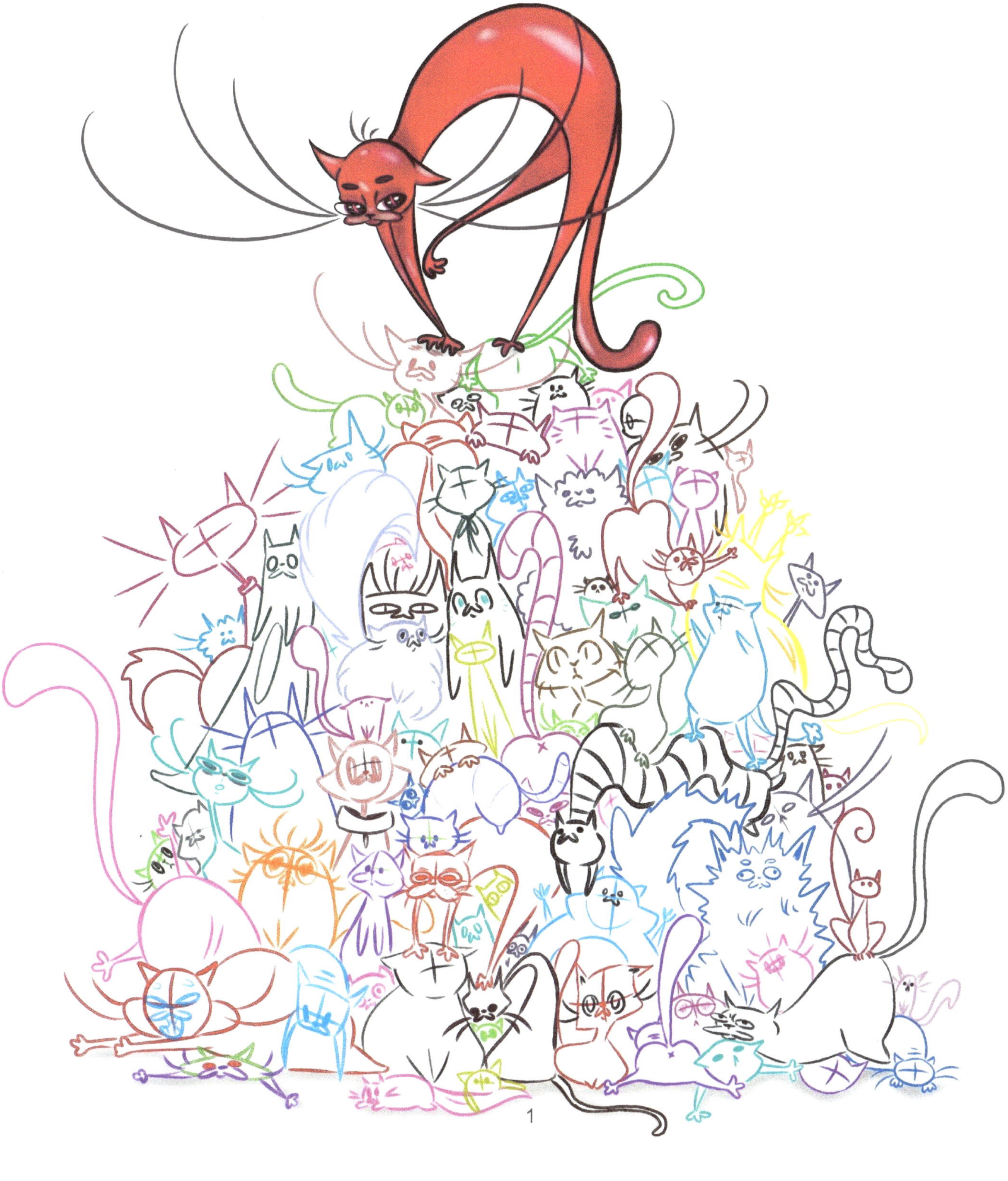

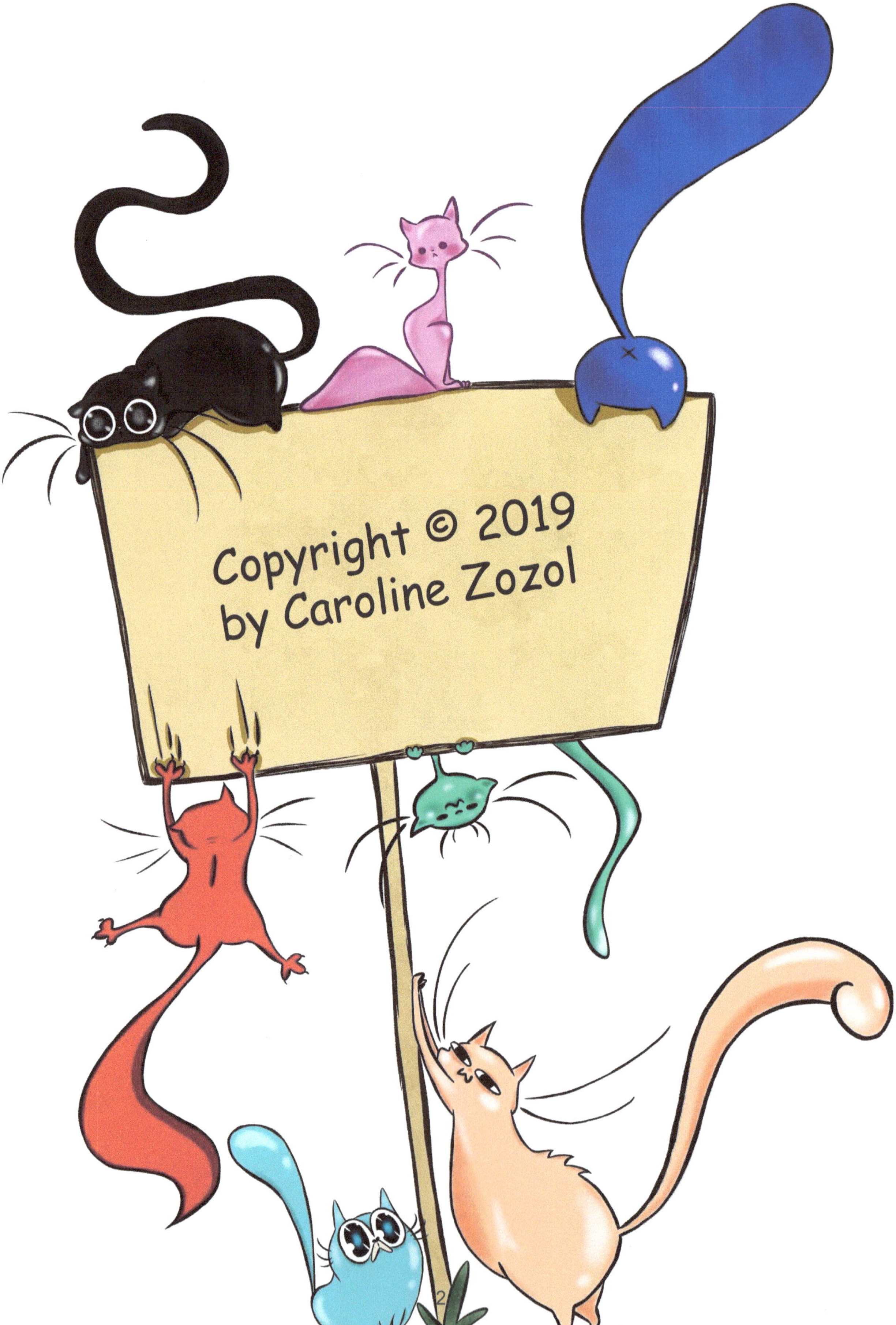
Copyright © 2019
by Caroline Zozol

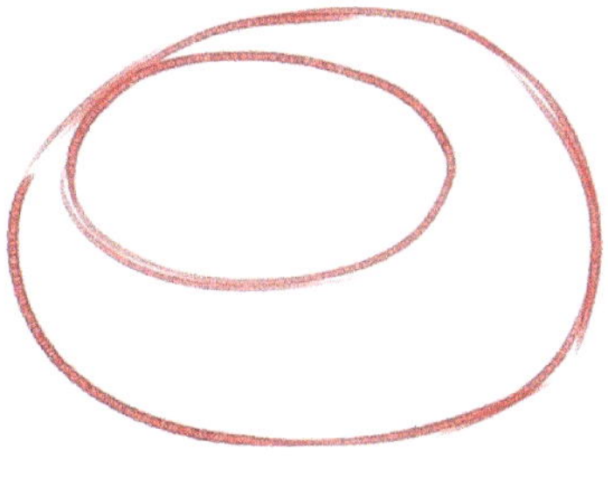

Always start the drawing using pencil, and have the eraser nearby!

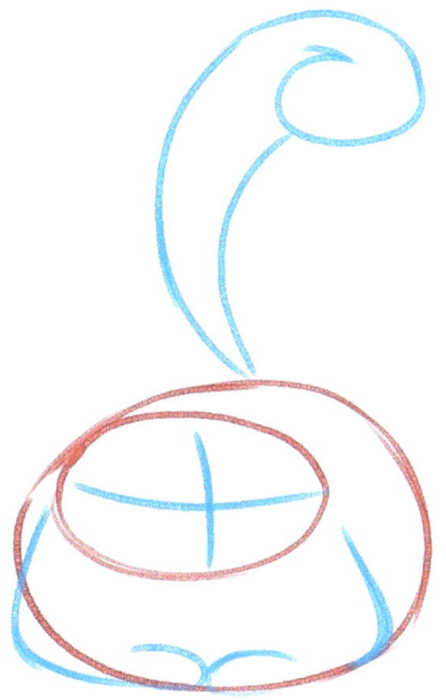

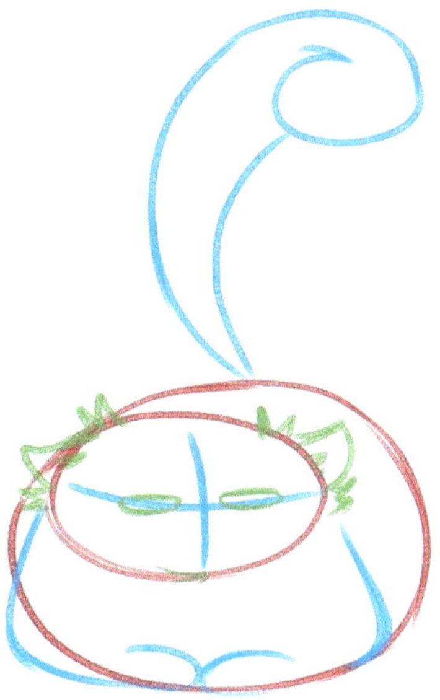

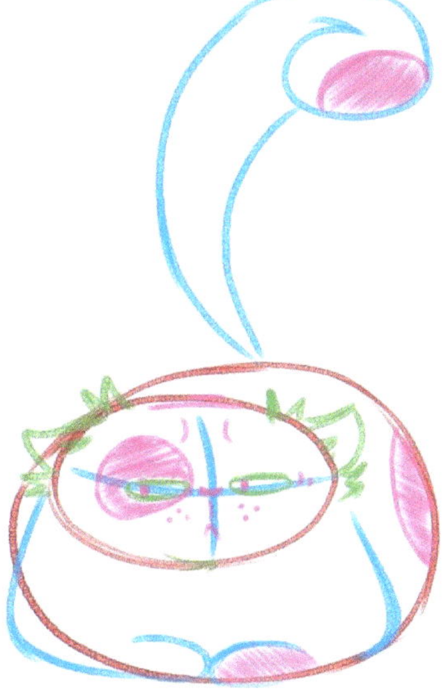

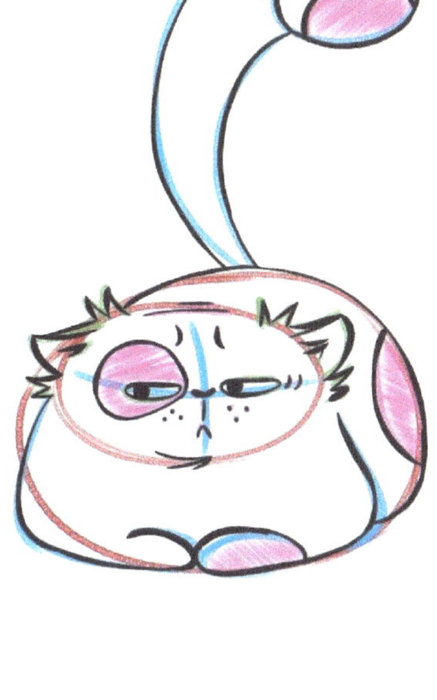

Trace the drawing with a black pen and erase it after you're done

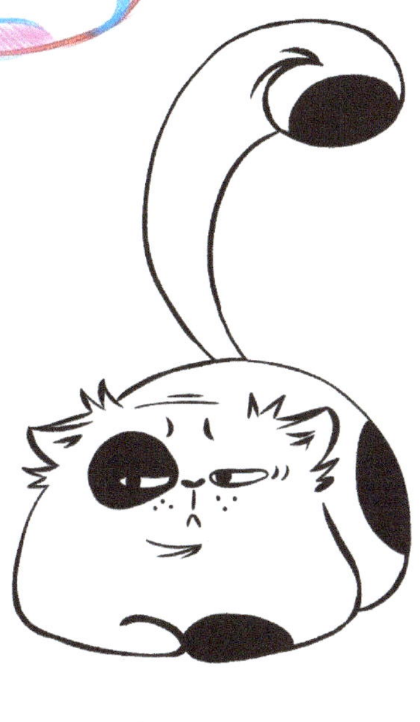

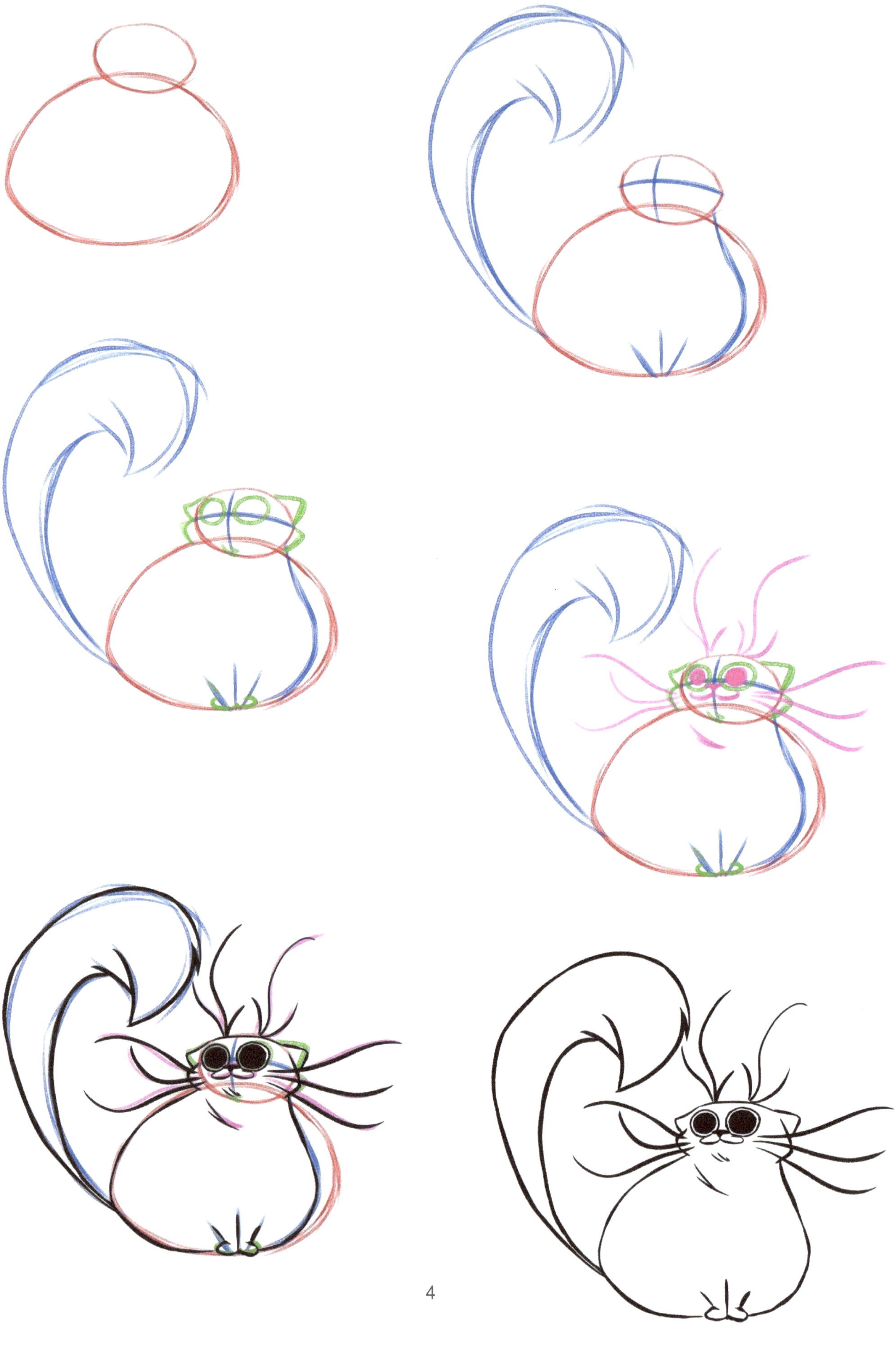

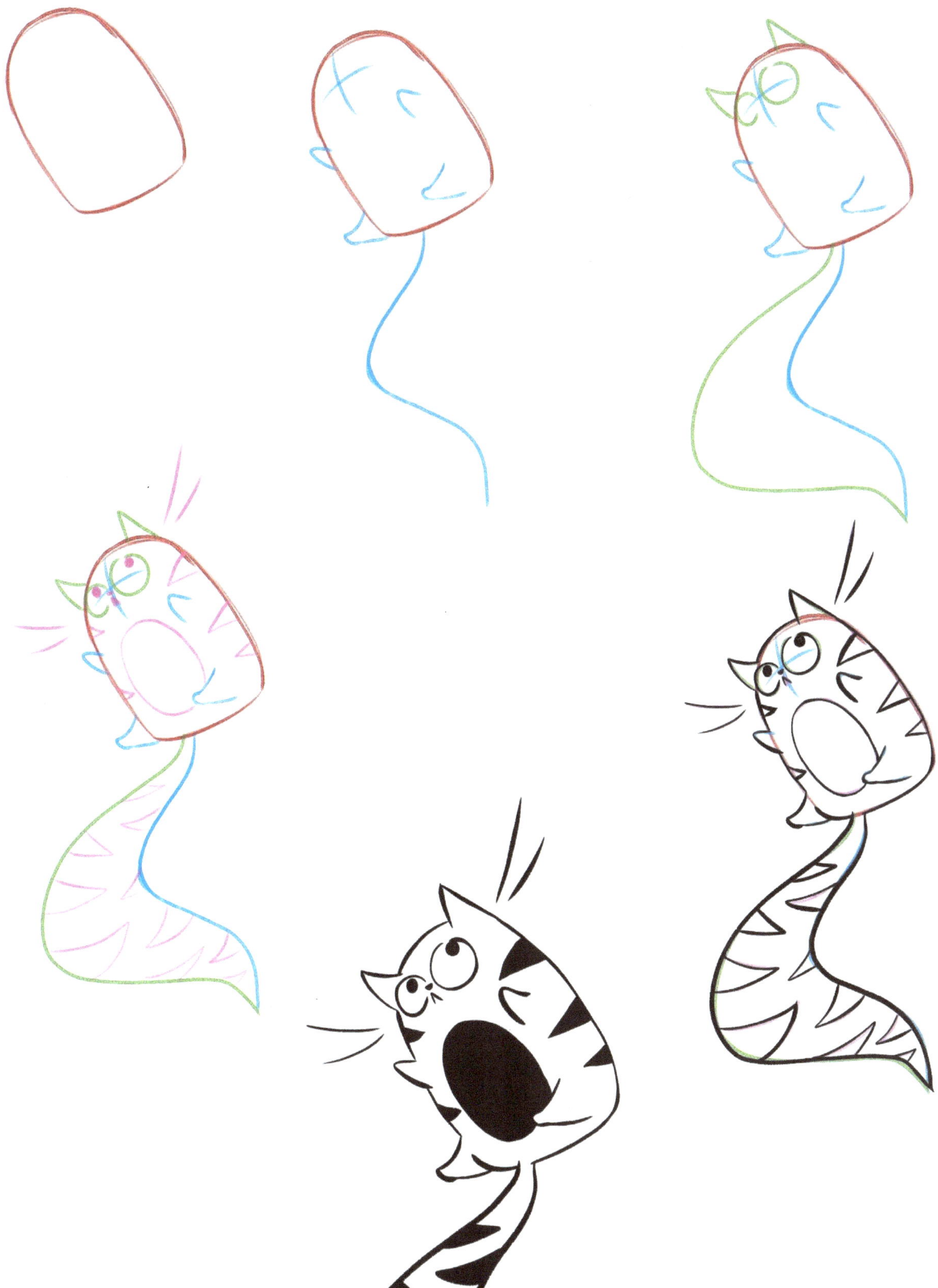

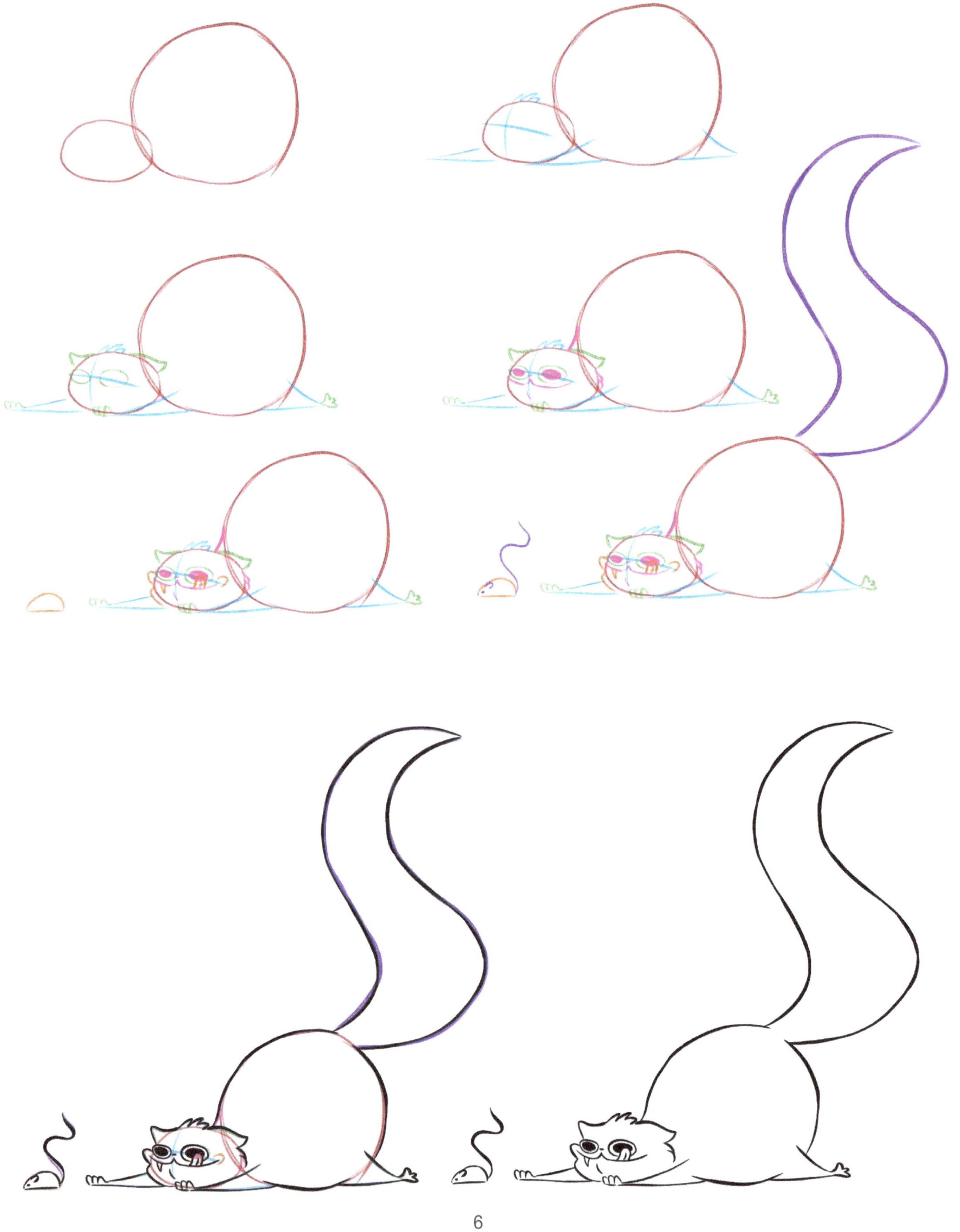

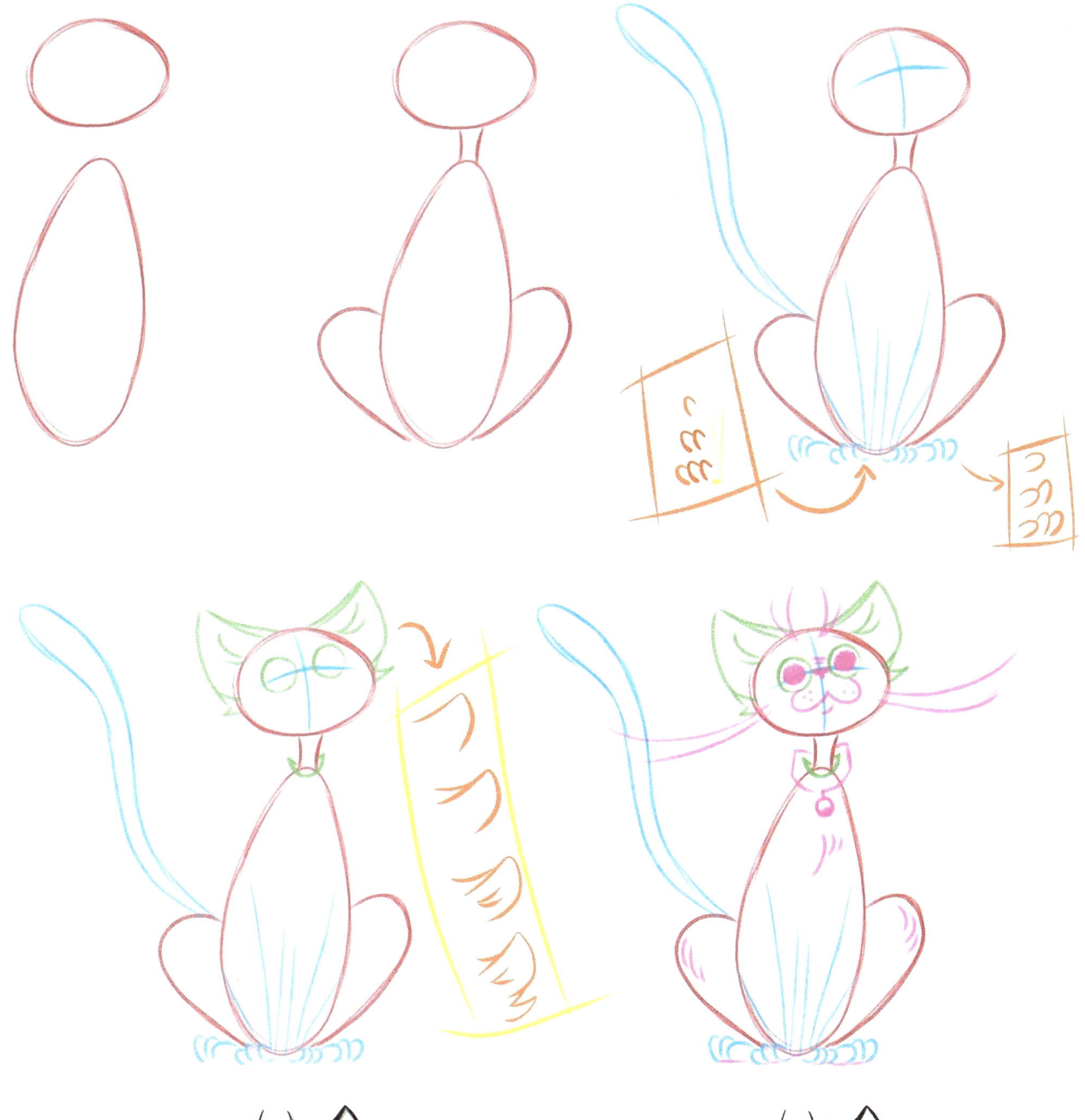

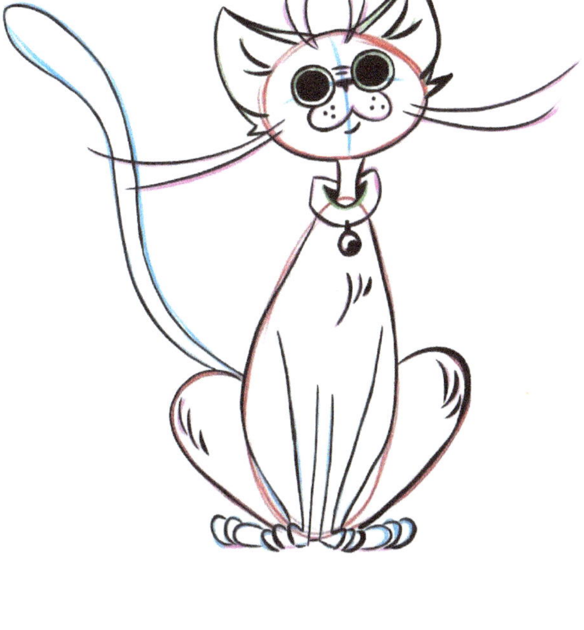

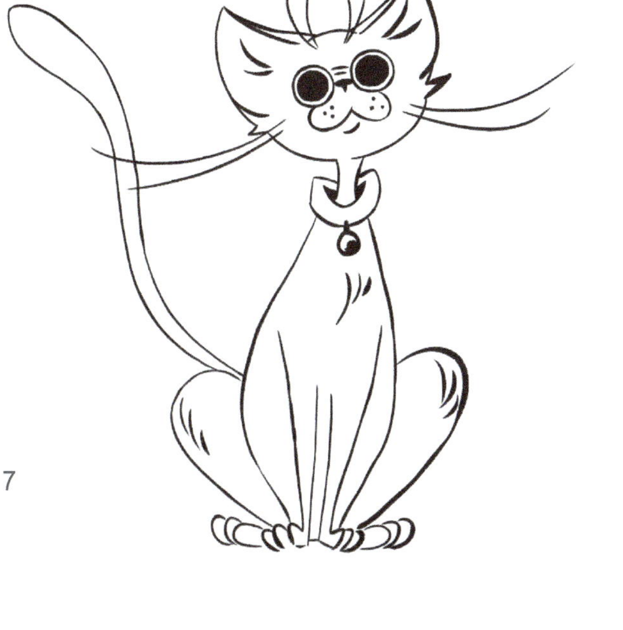

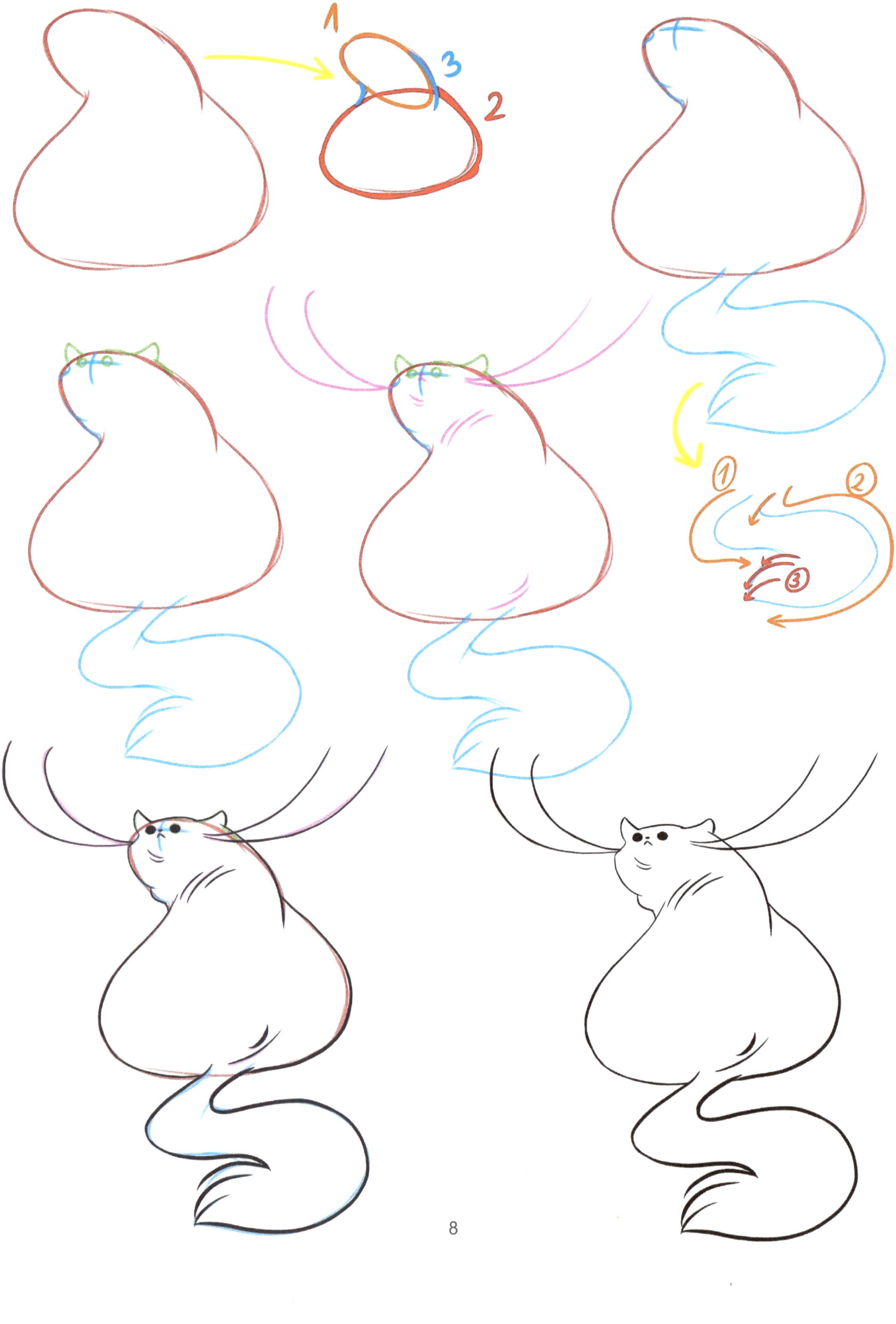
1
3
2
1
2
3

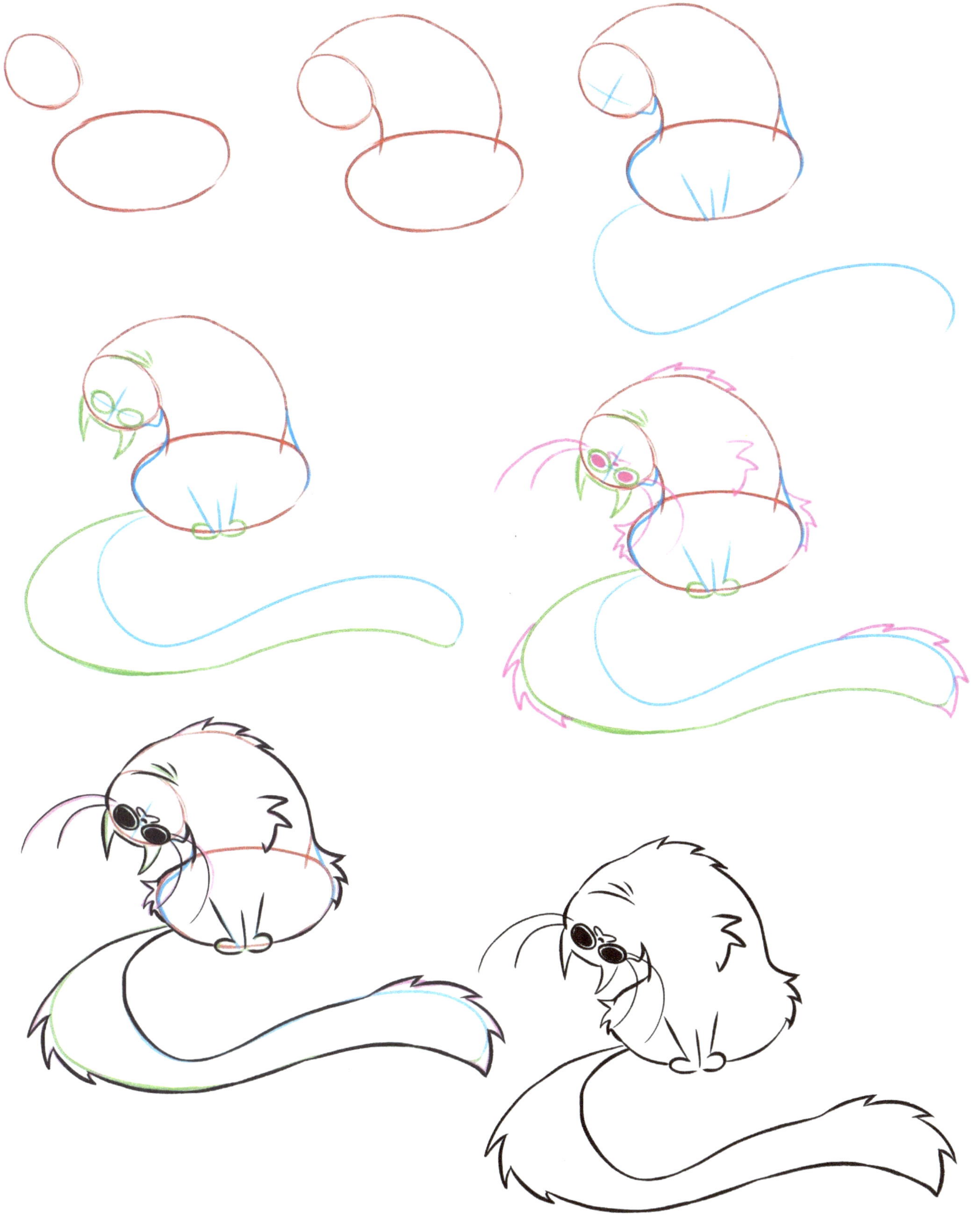

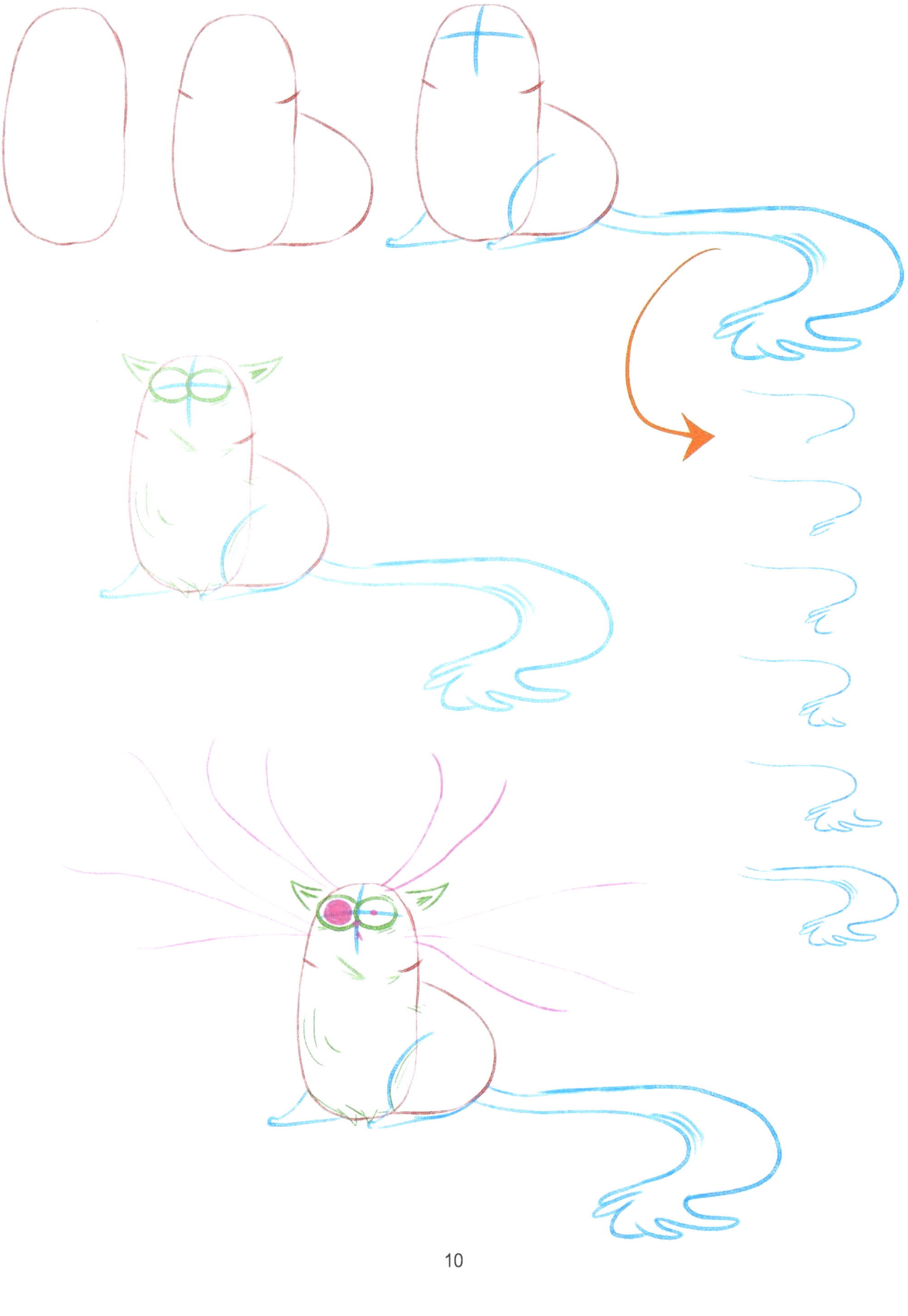

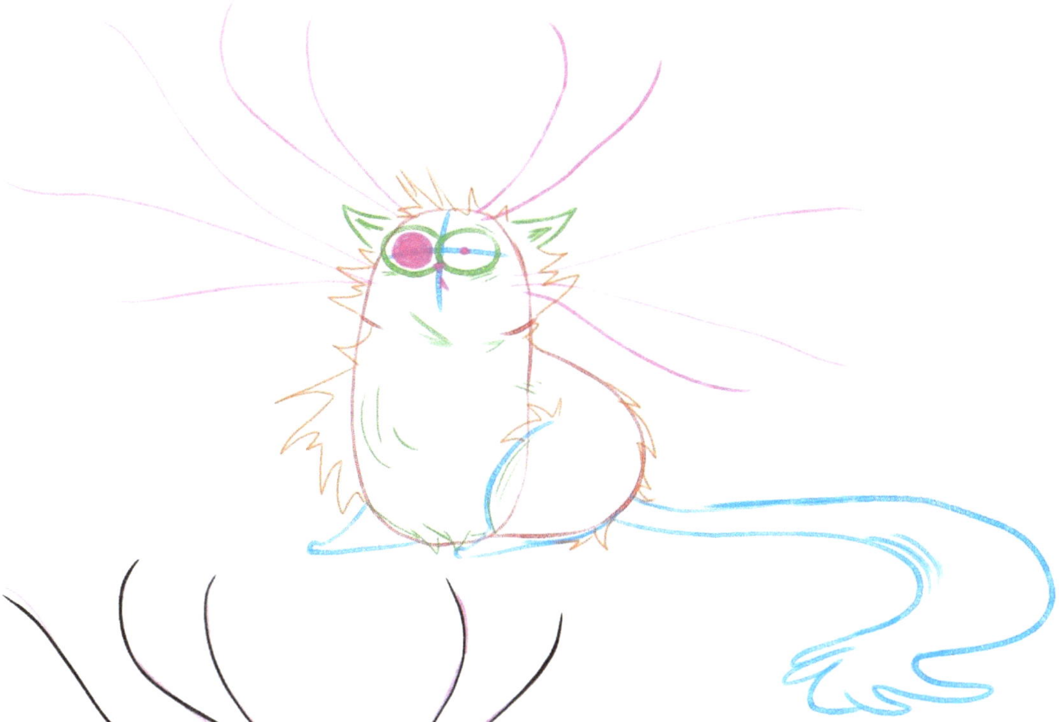

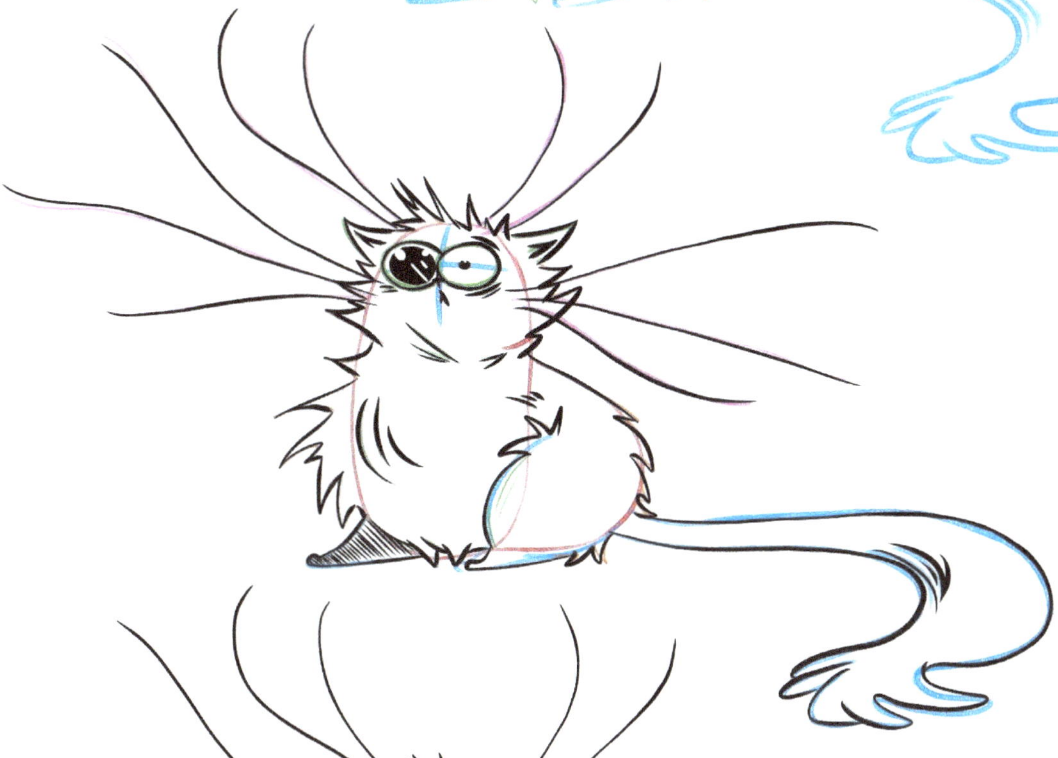

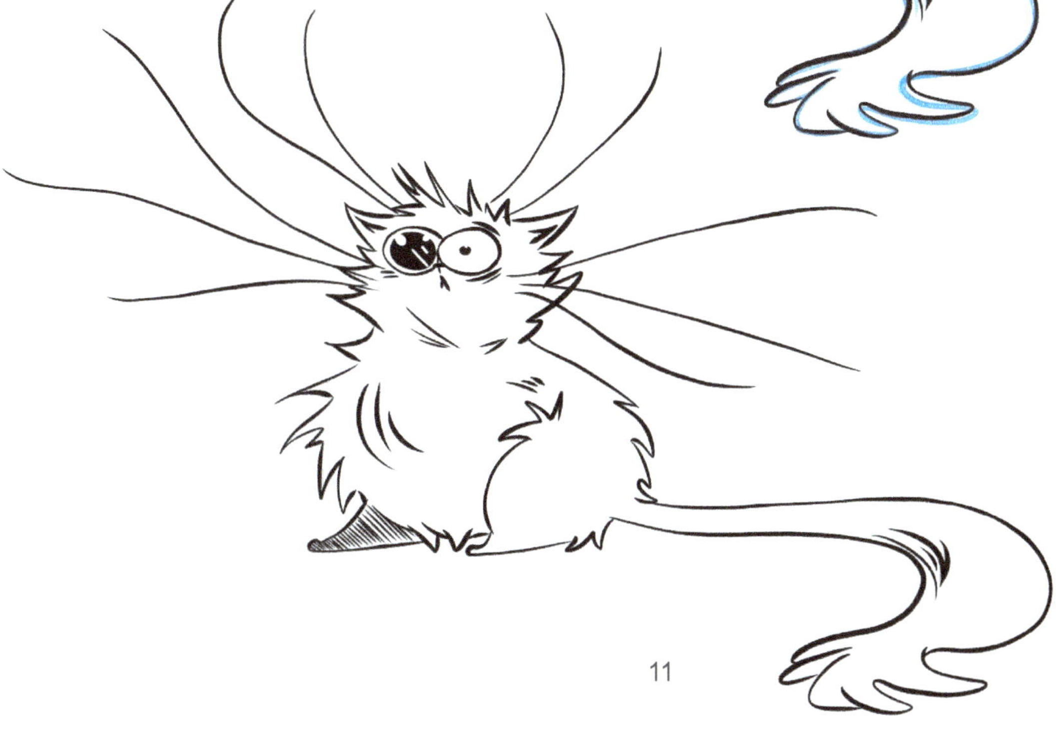

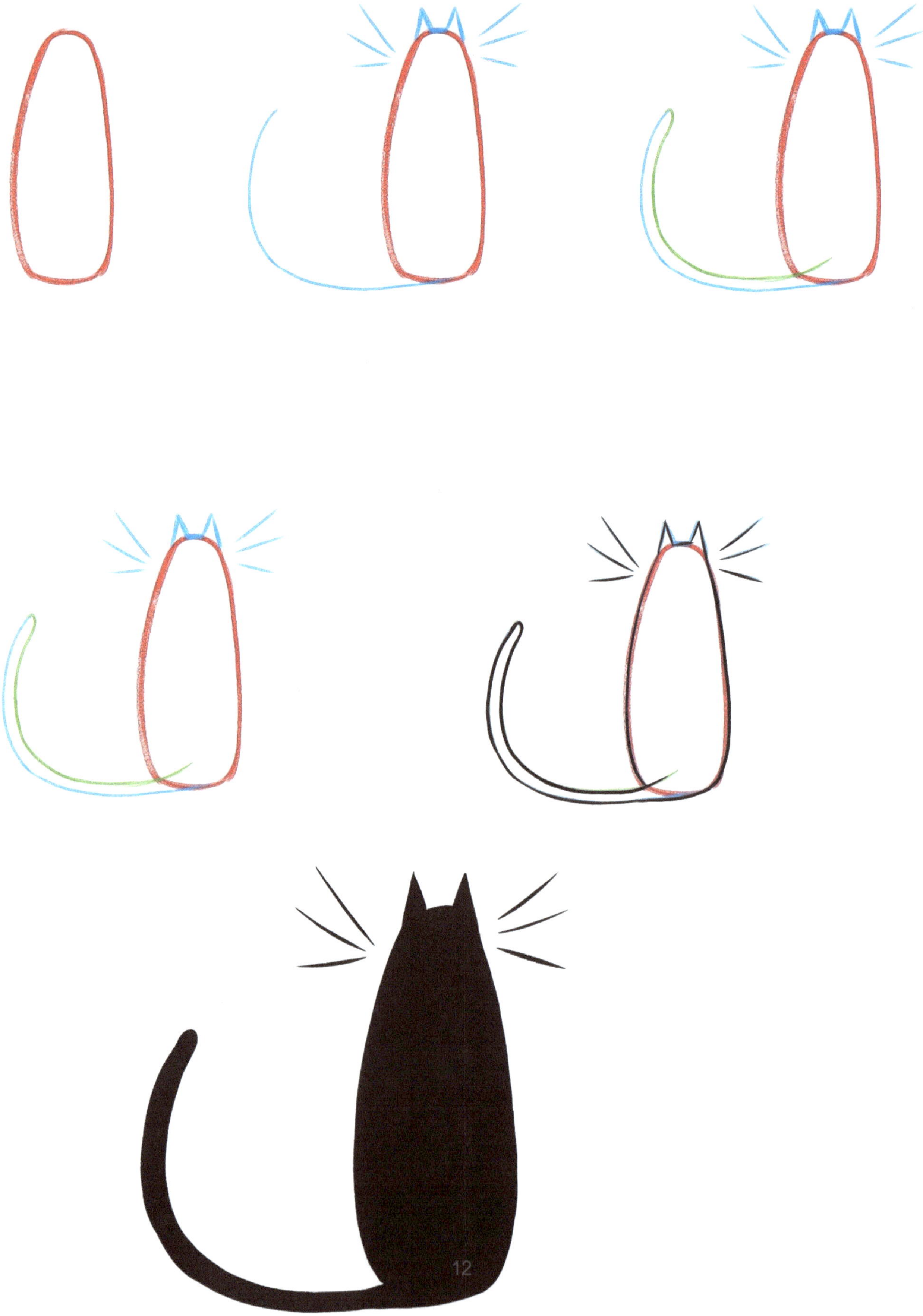

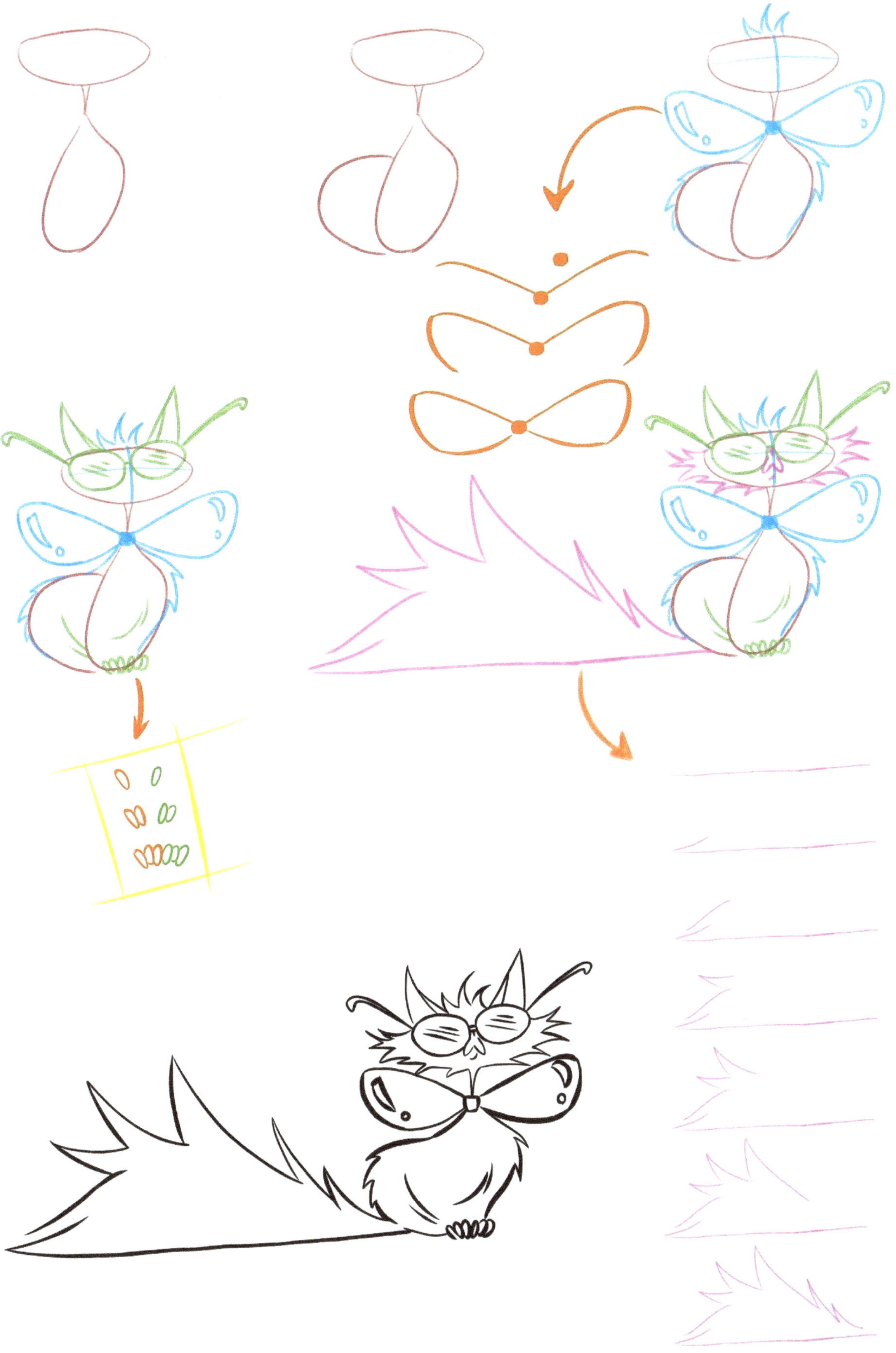

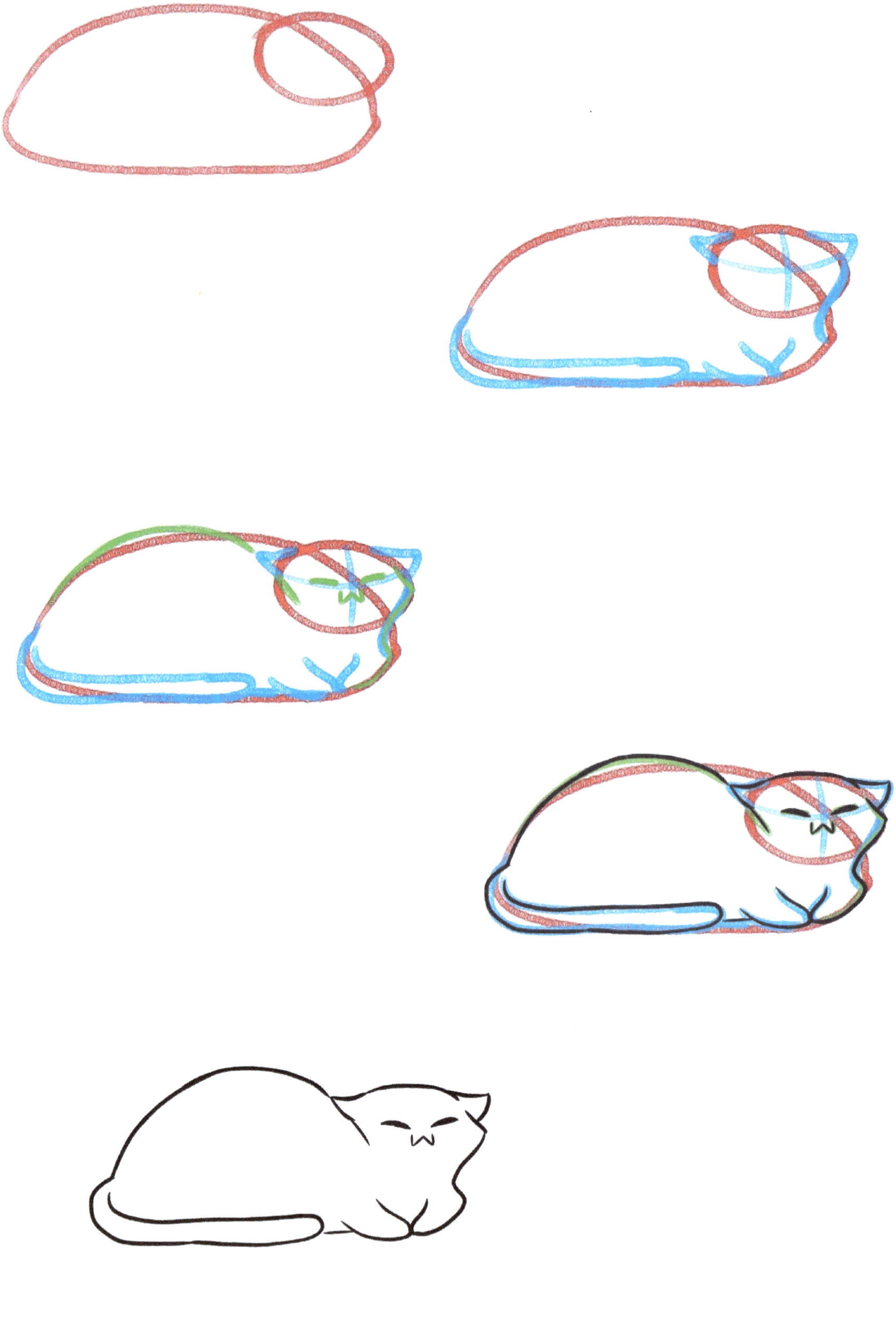

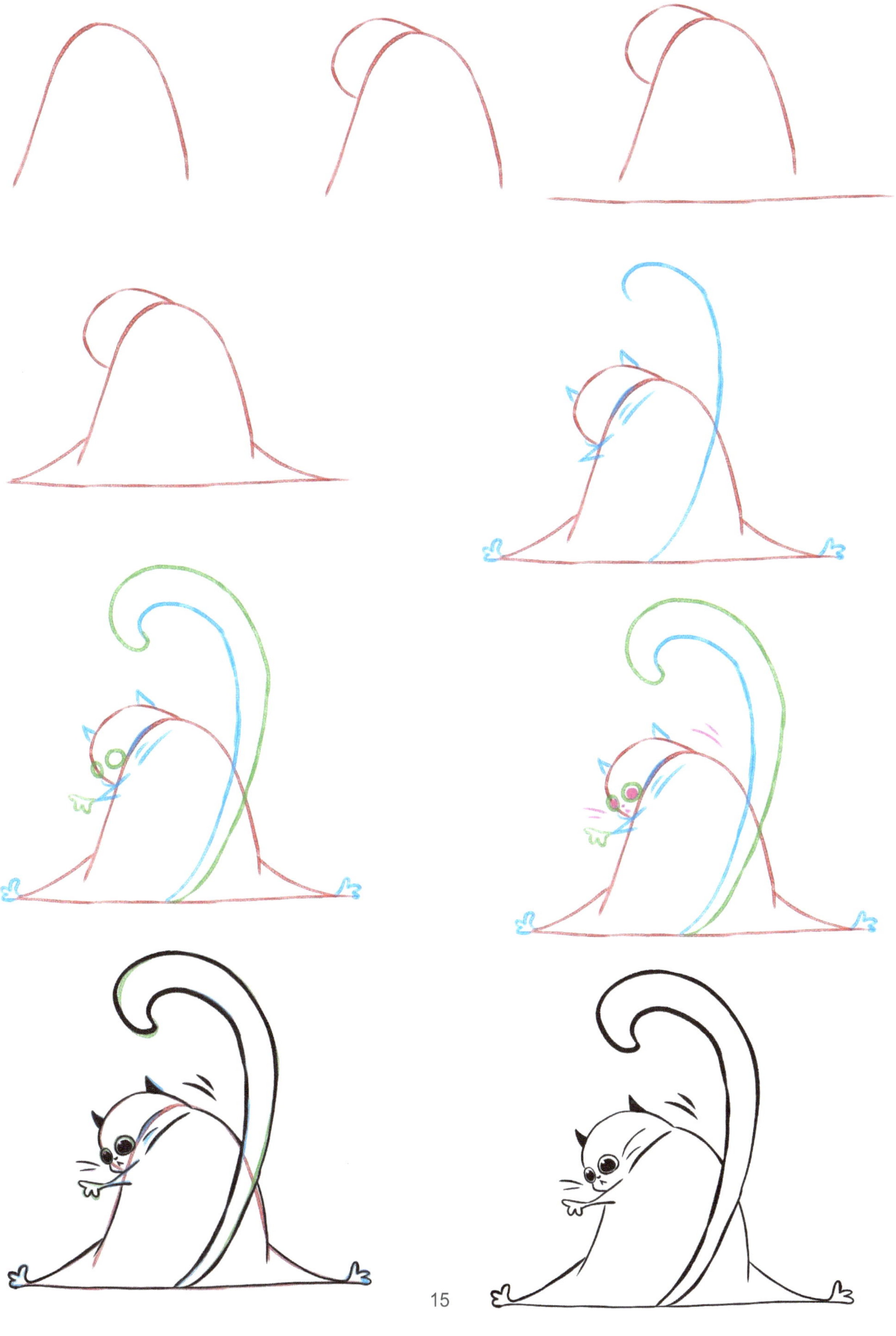

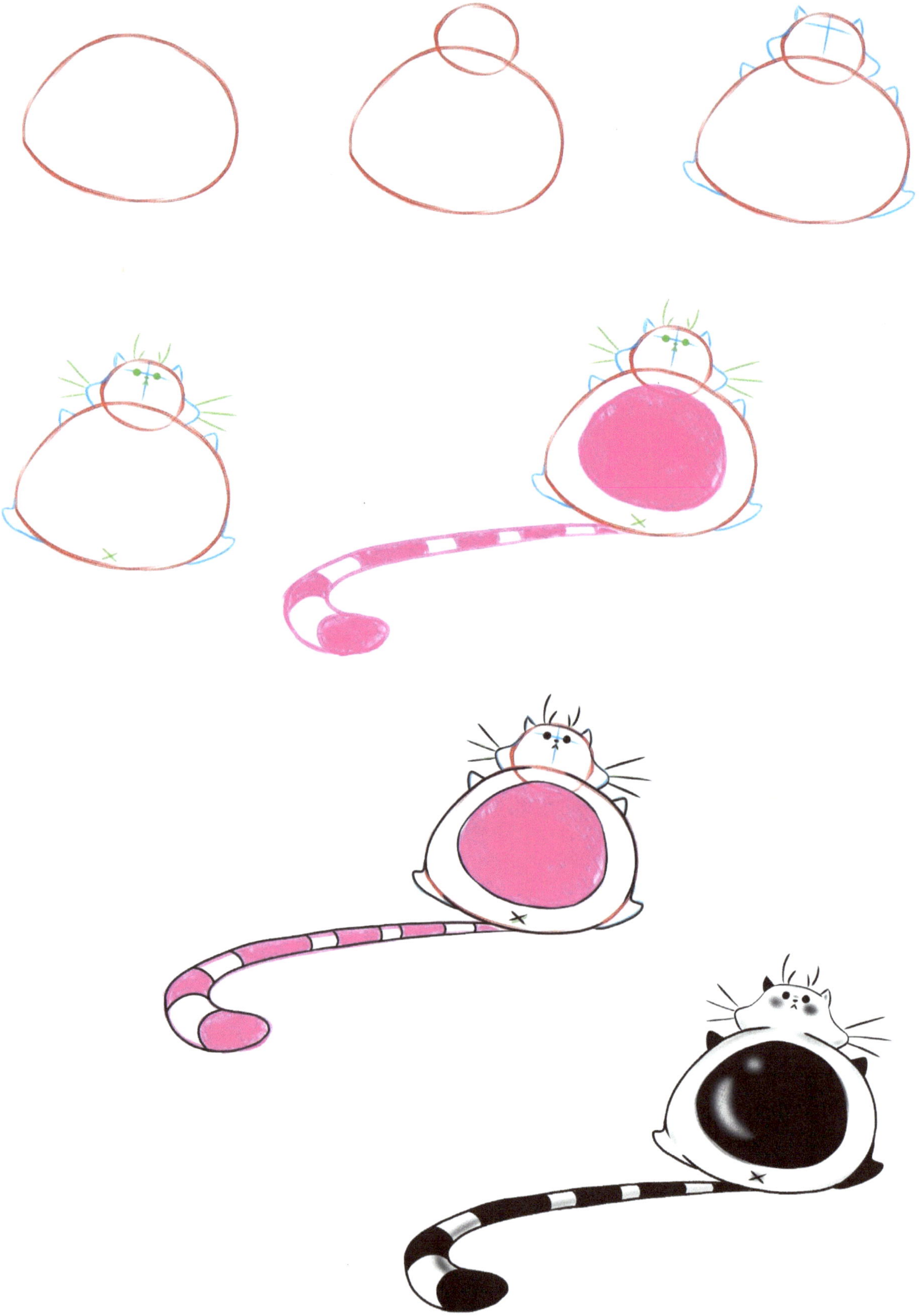

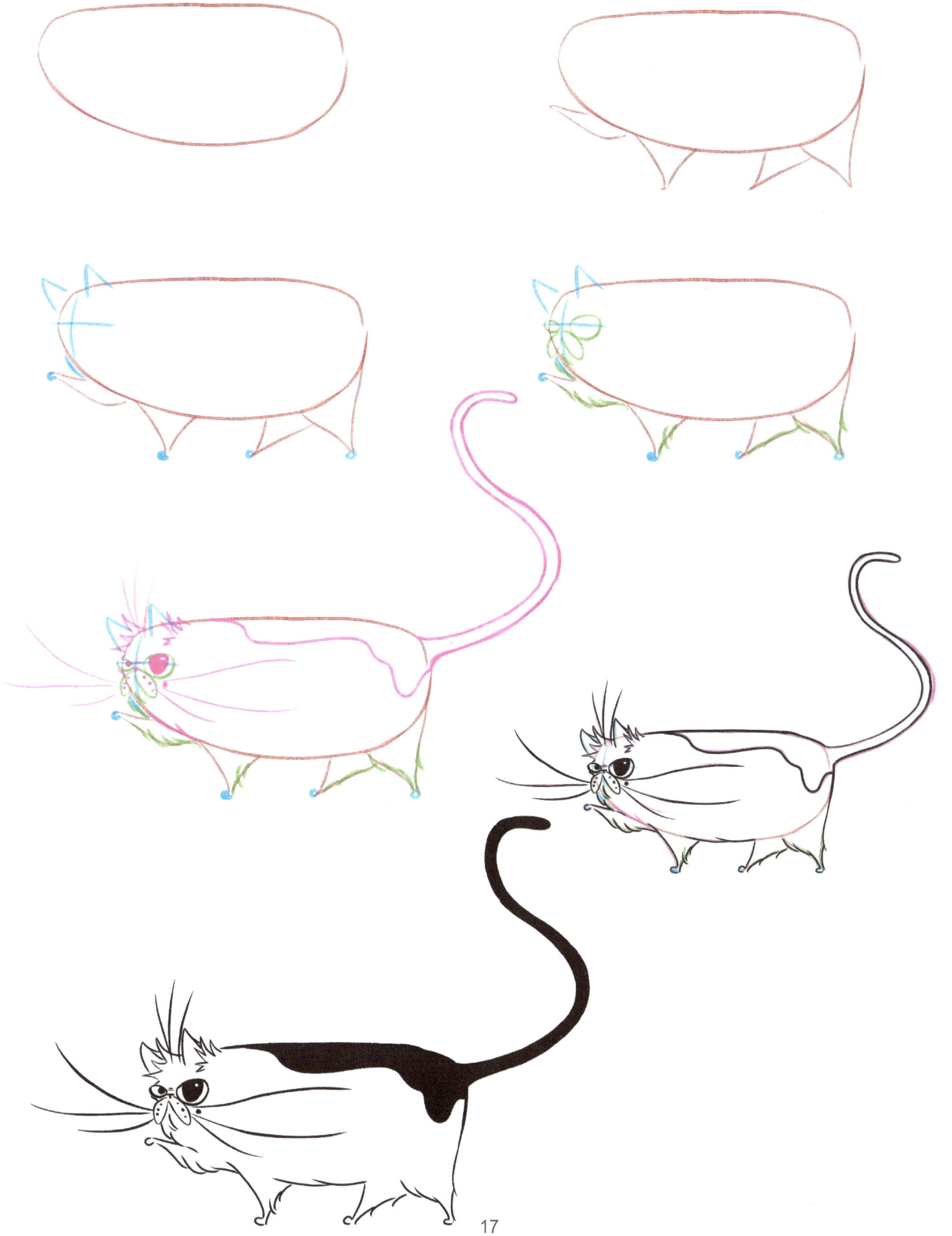

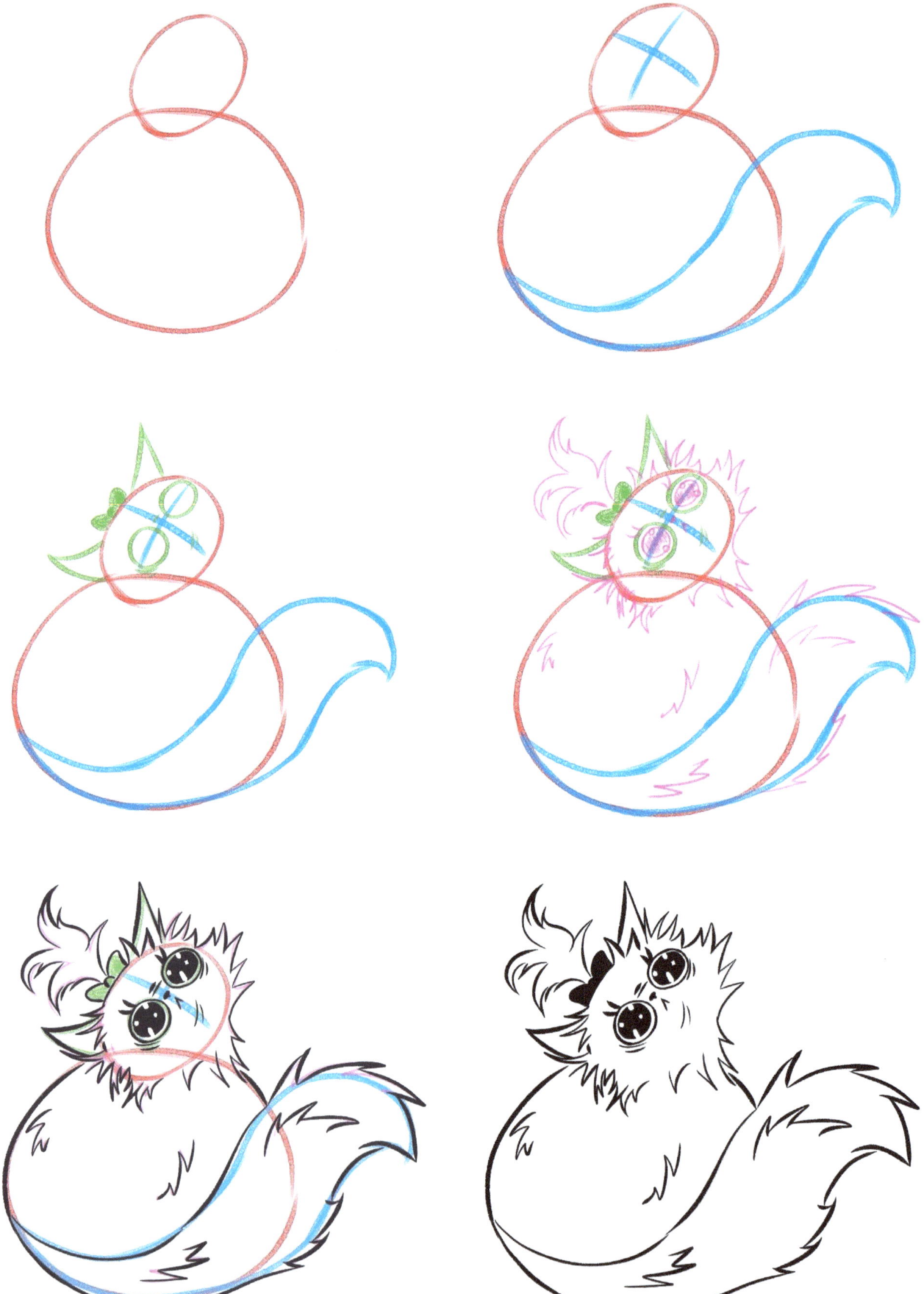

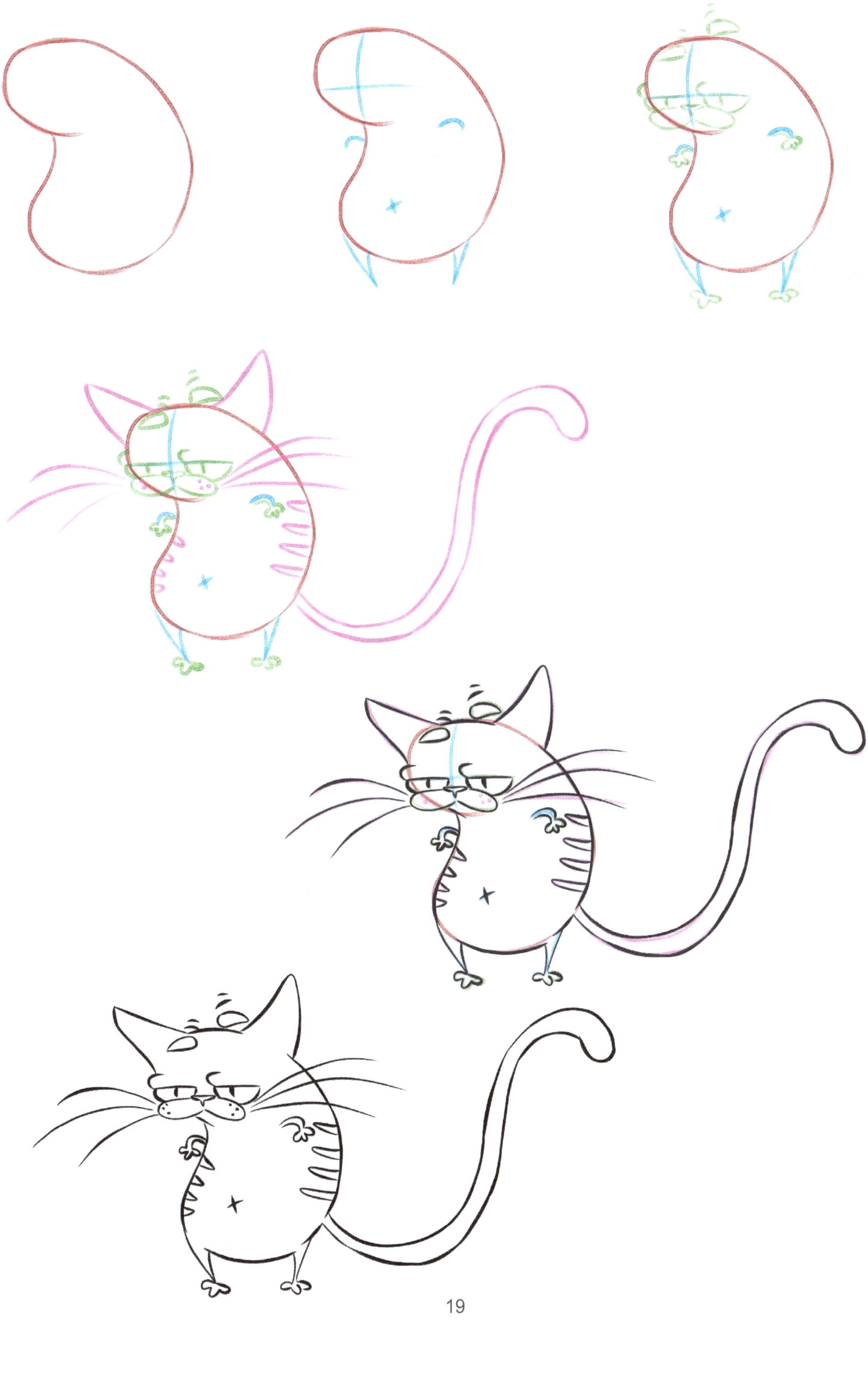

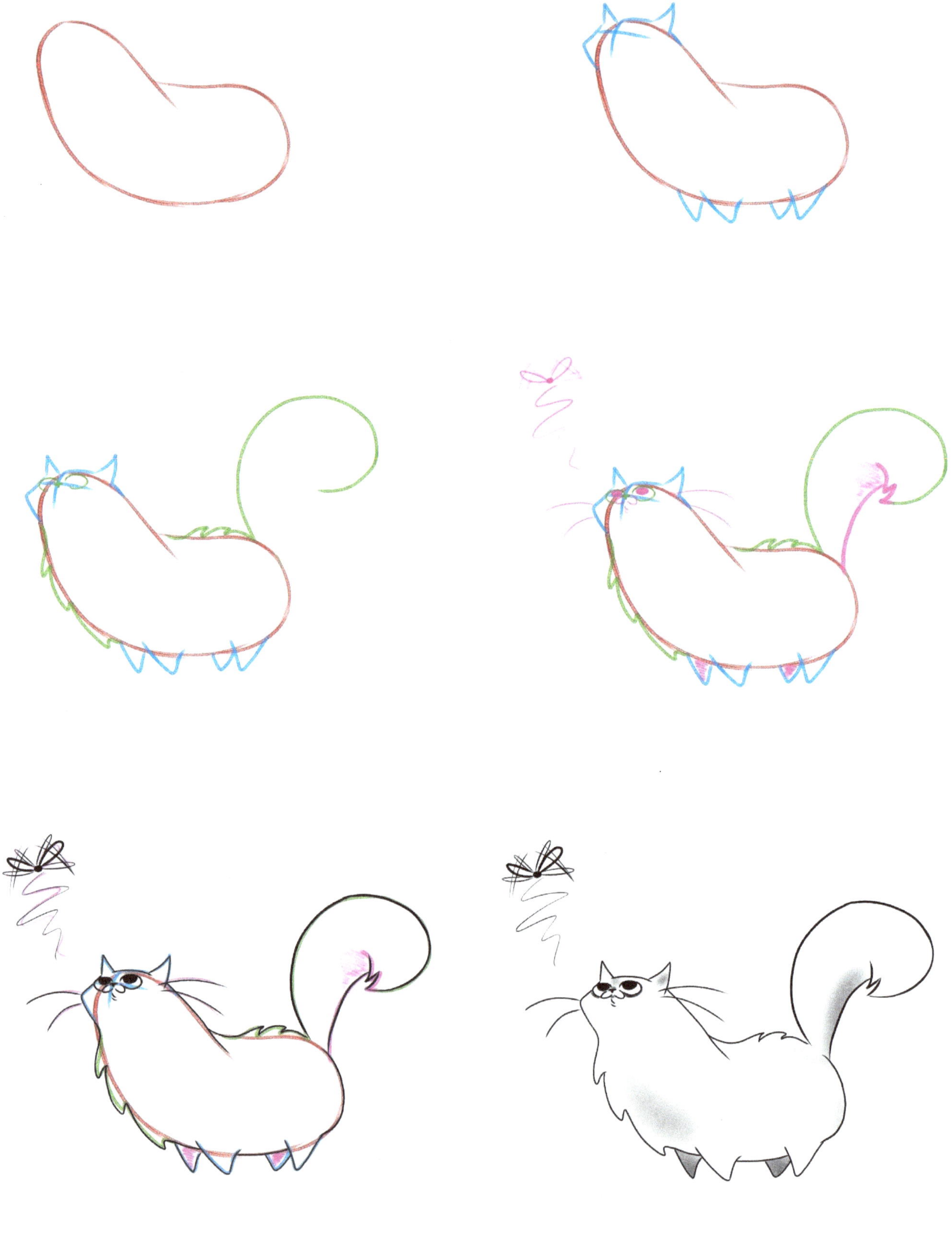

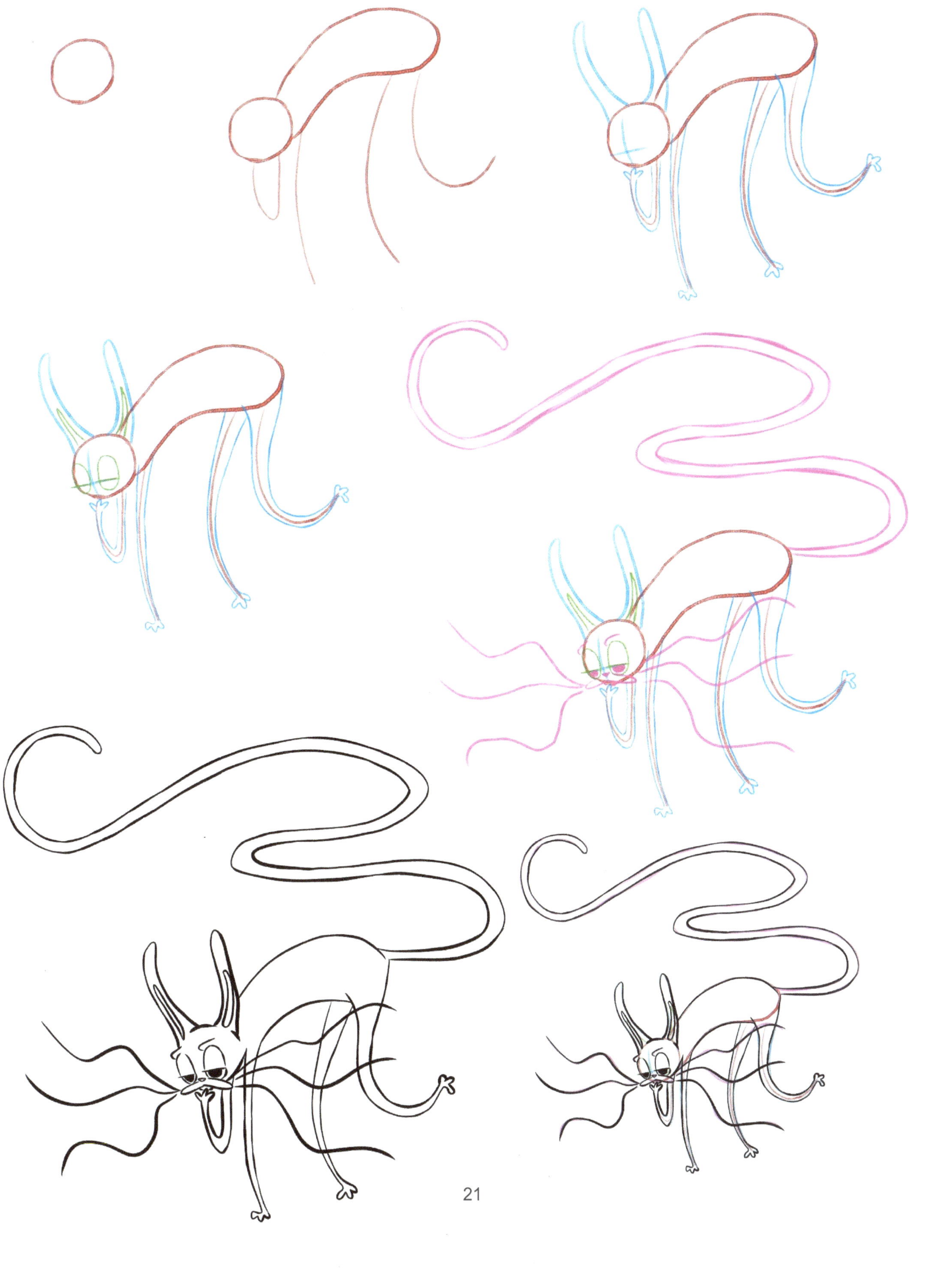

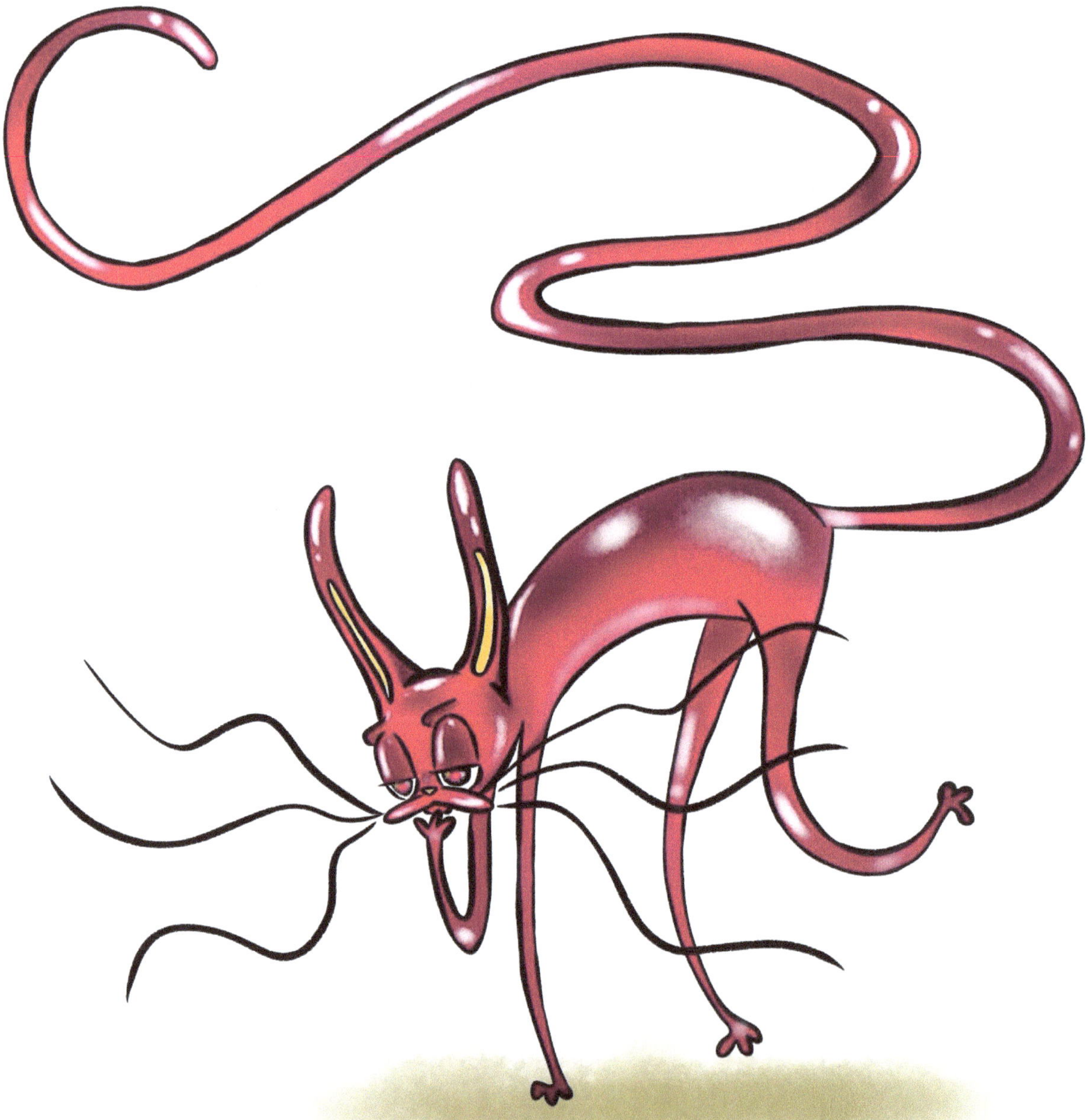

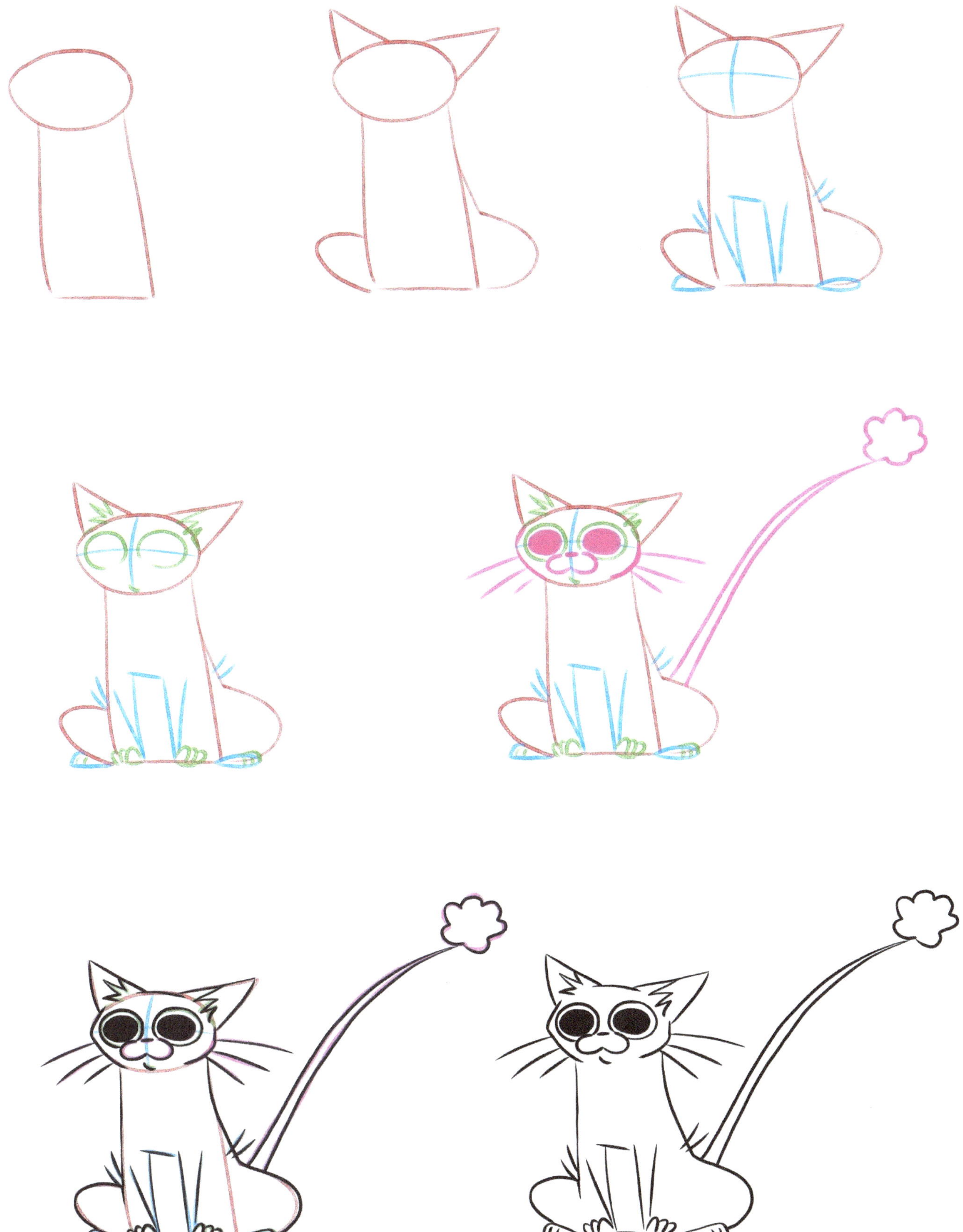

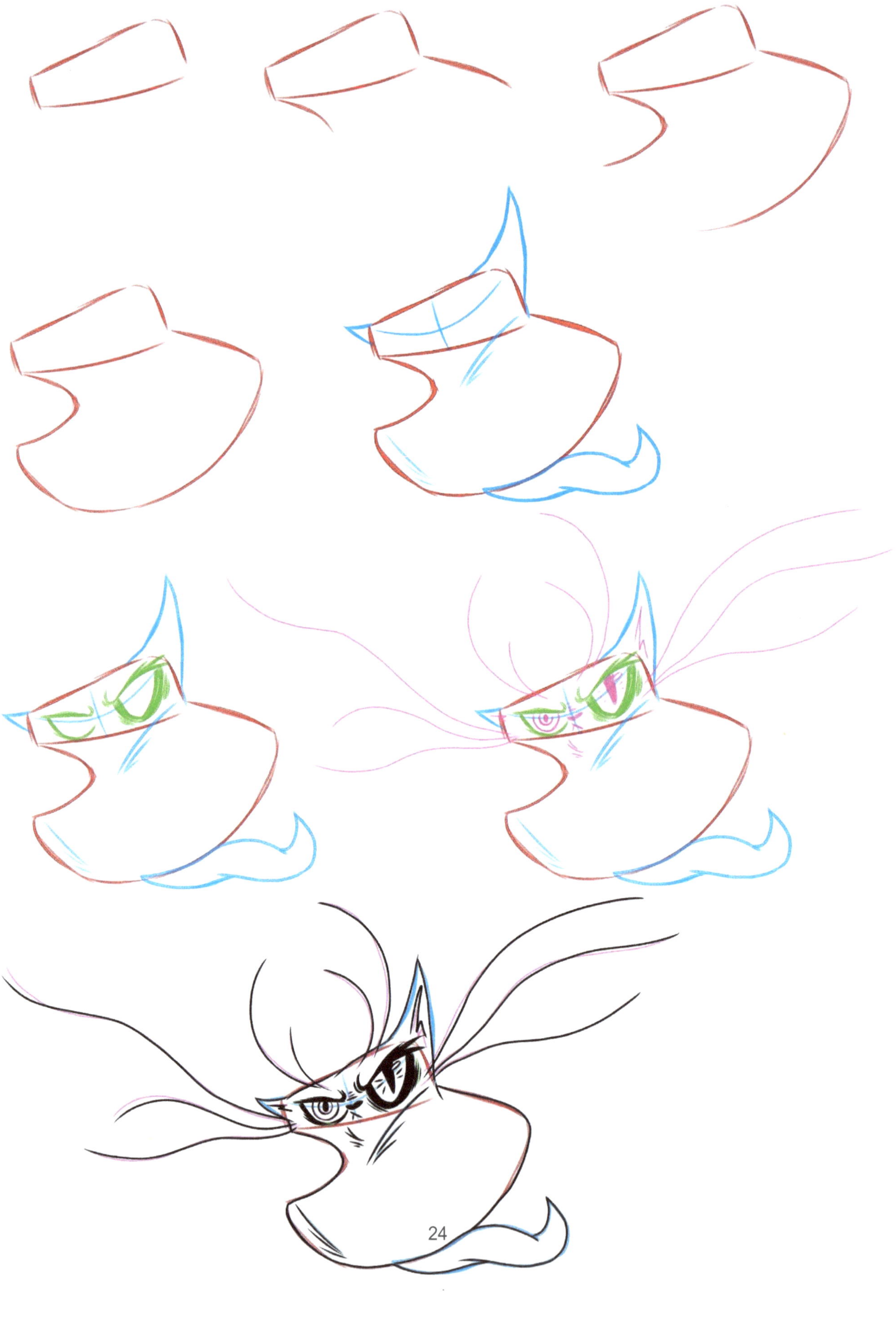

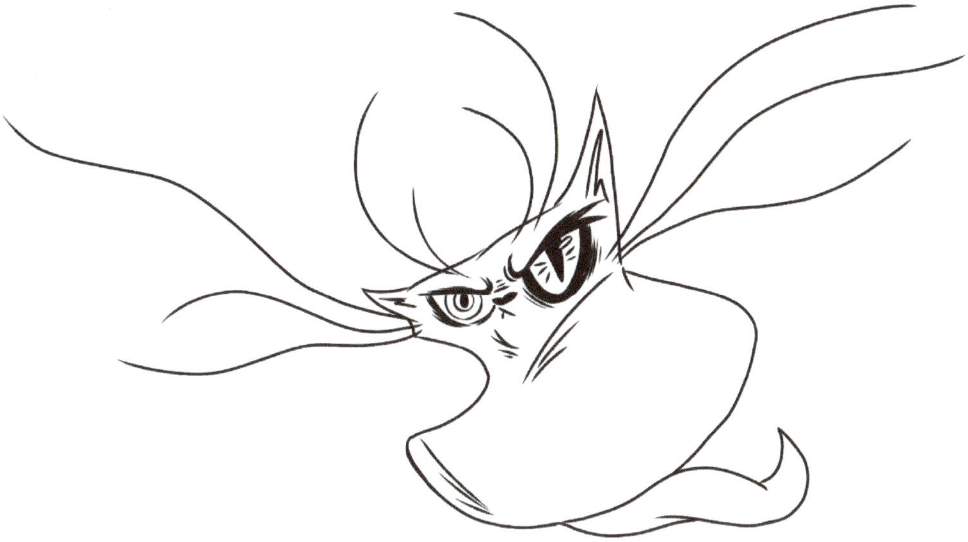

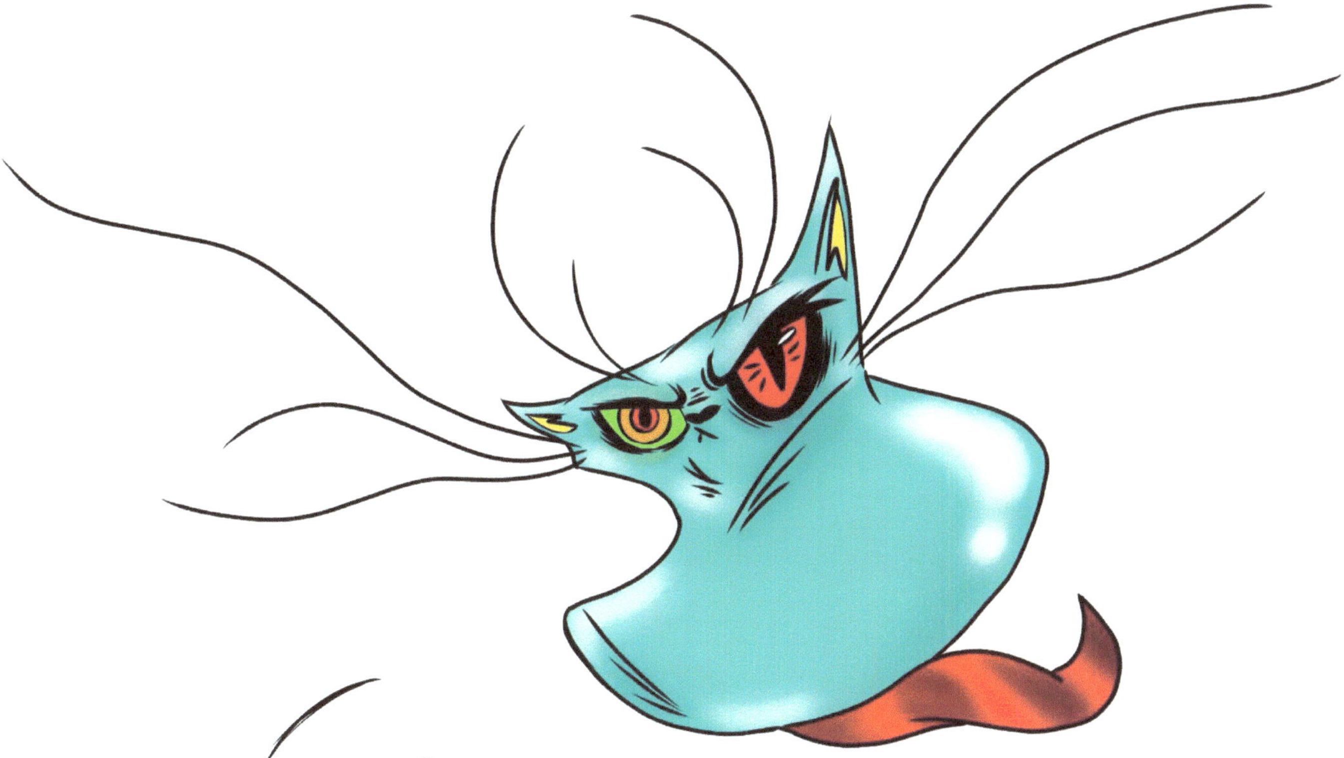

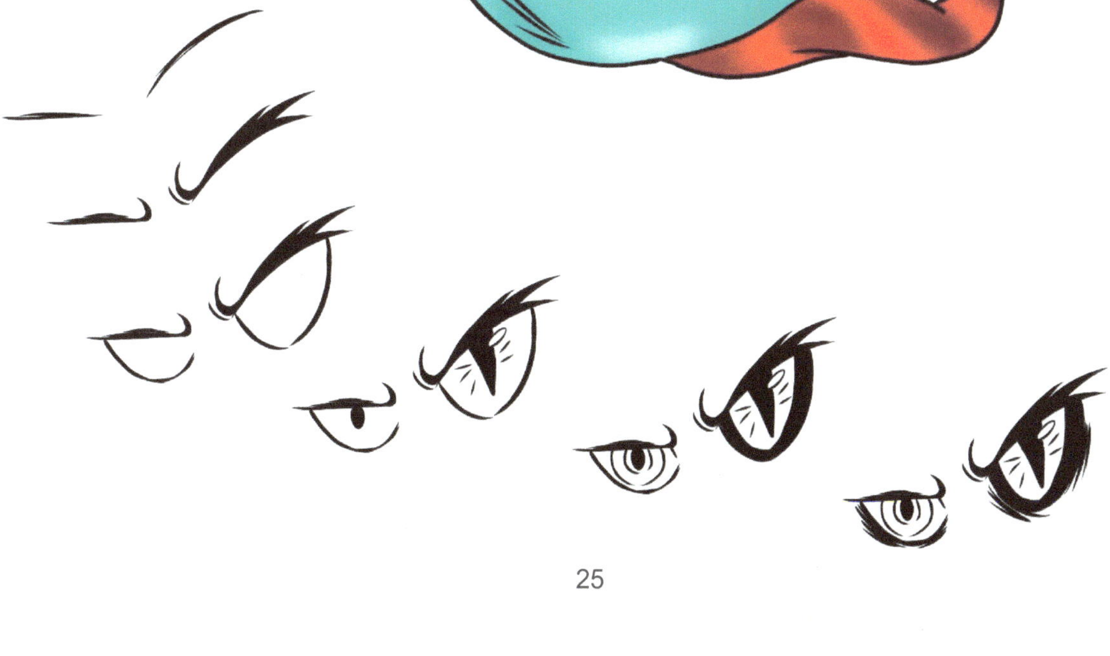

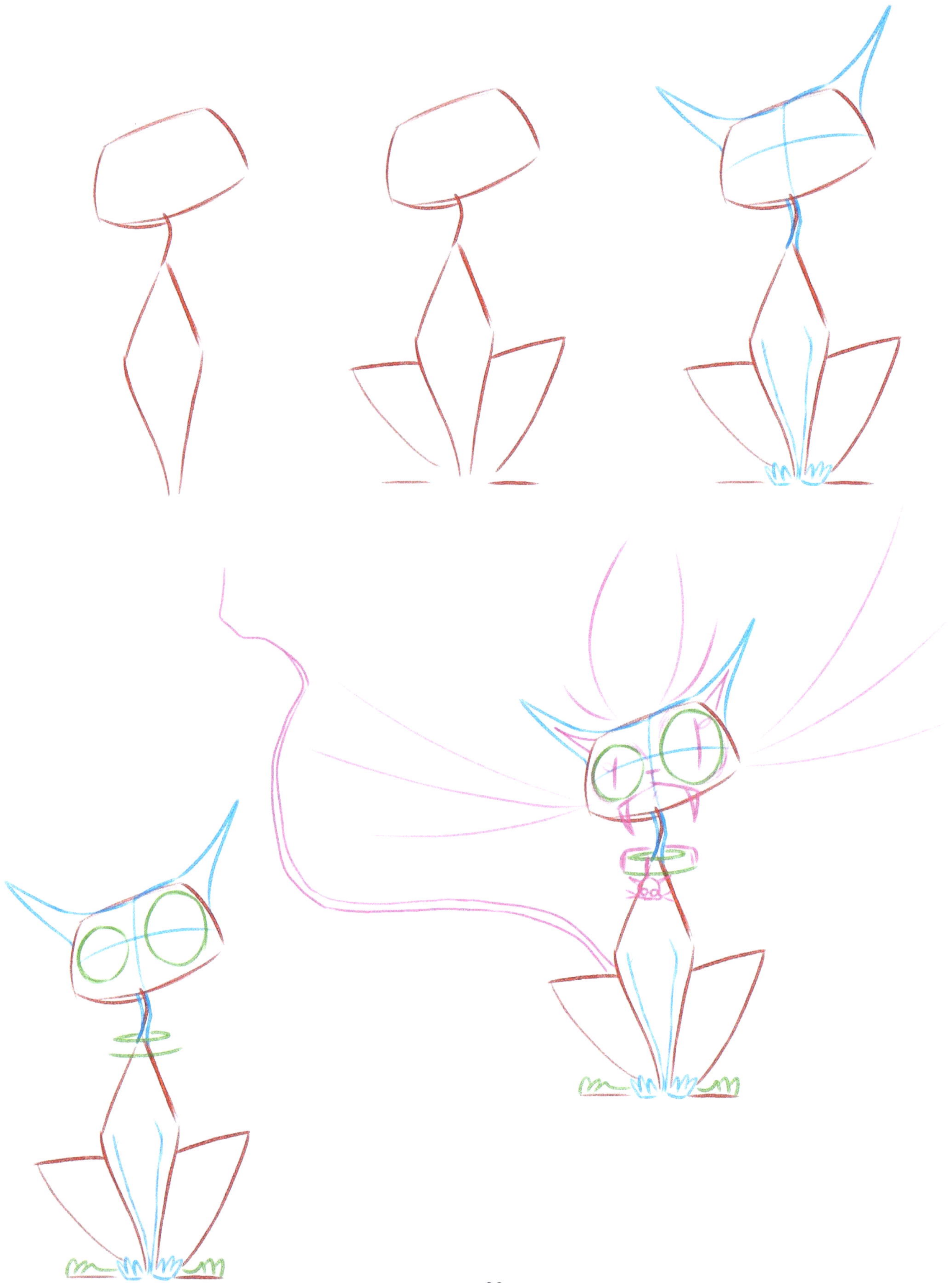

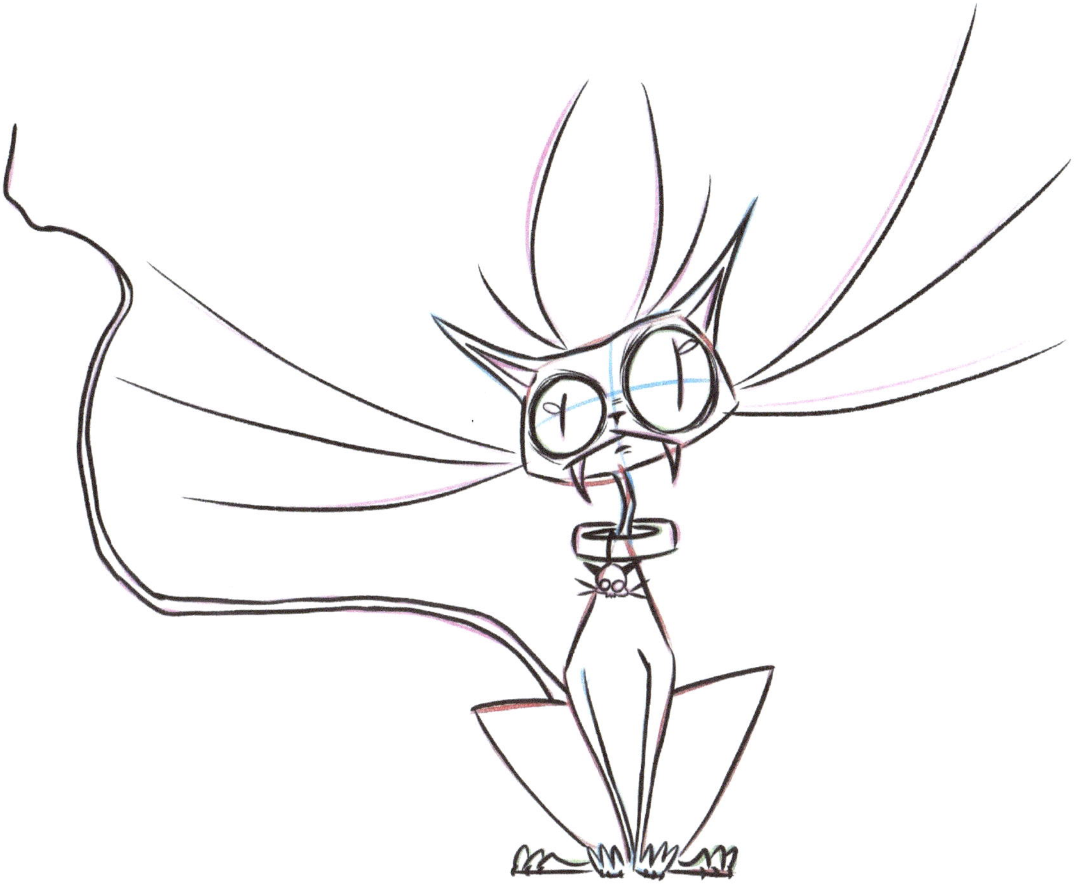

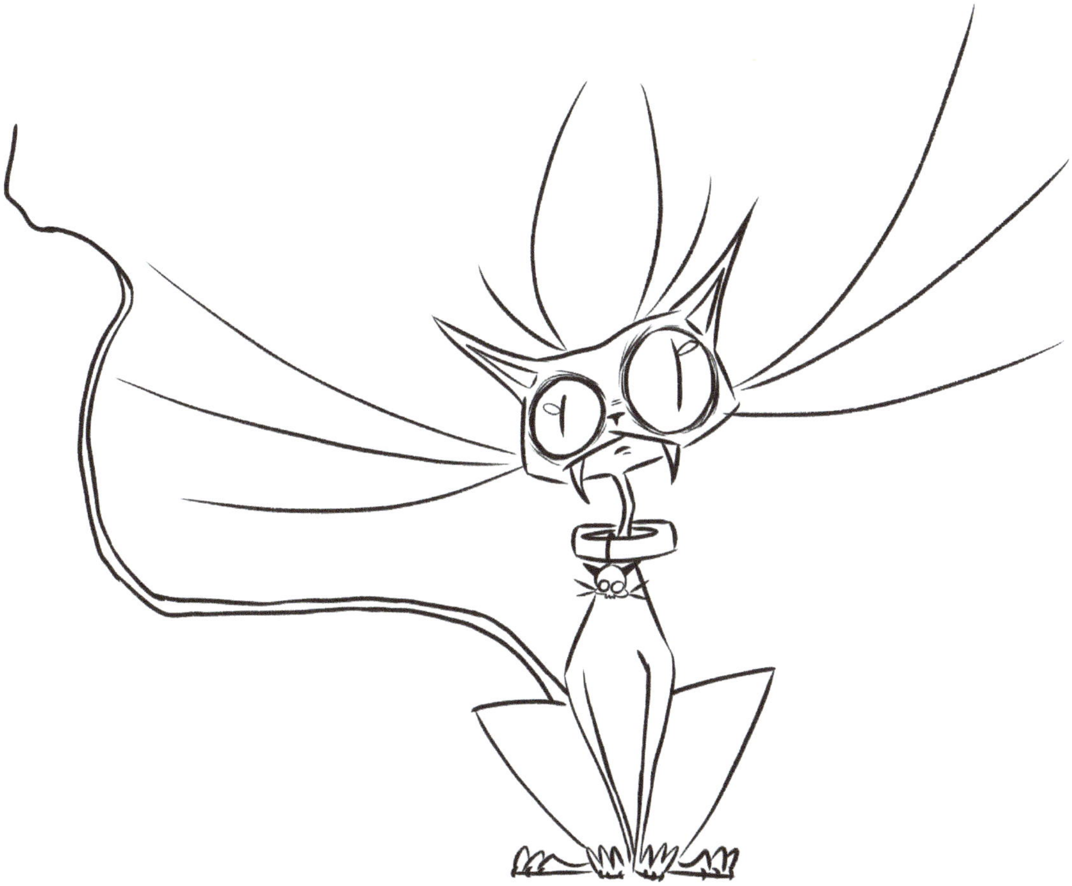

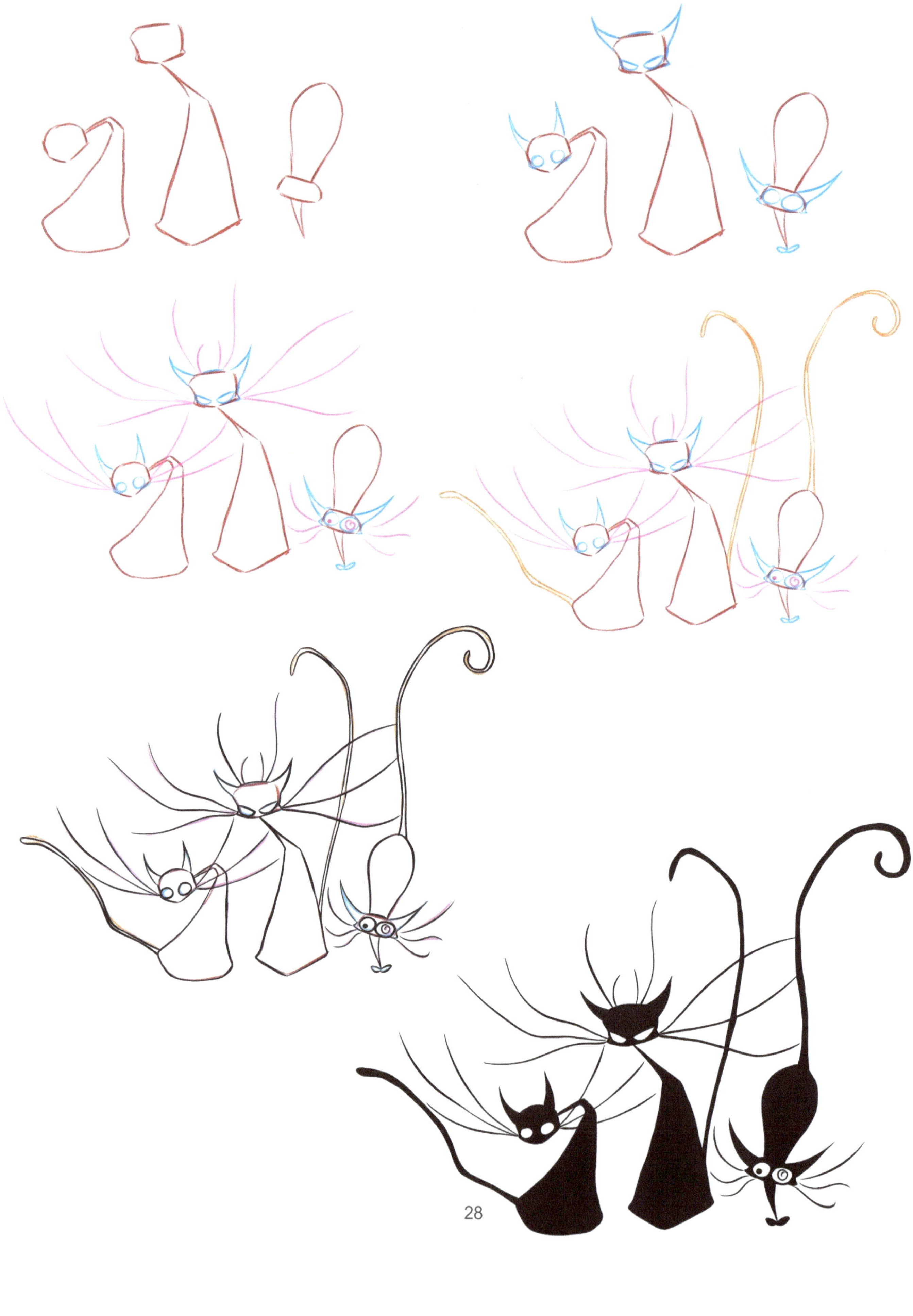

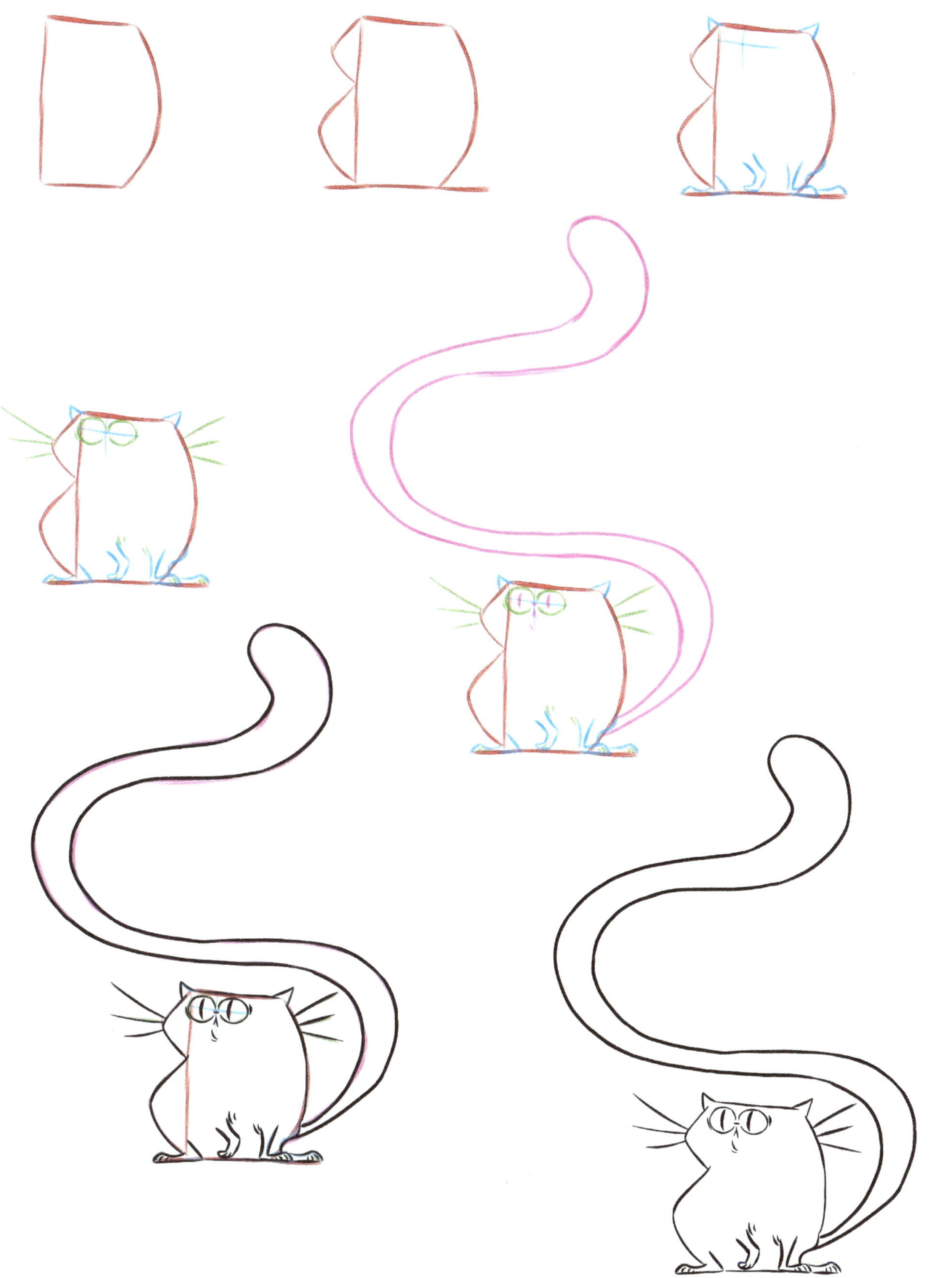

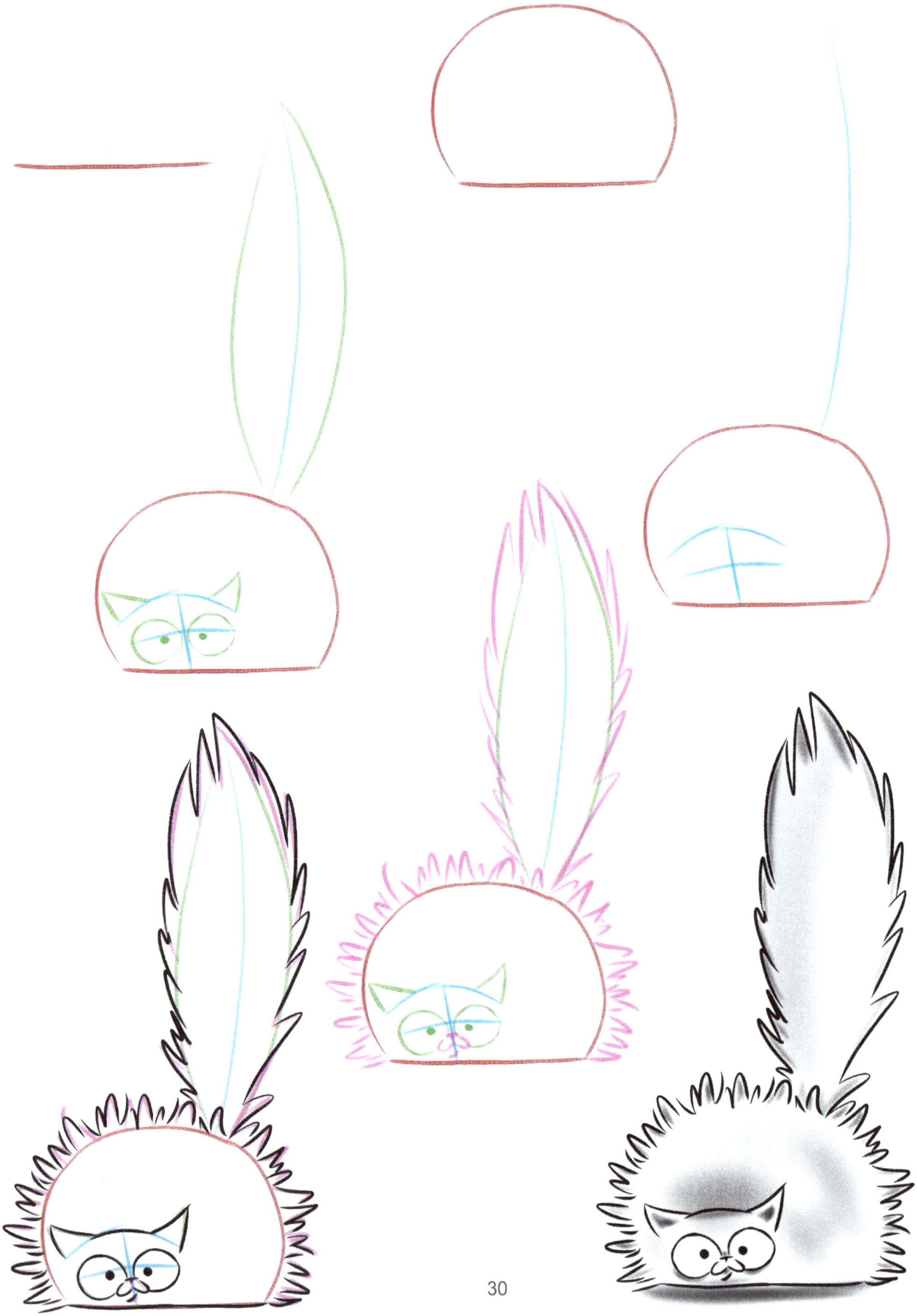

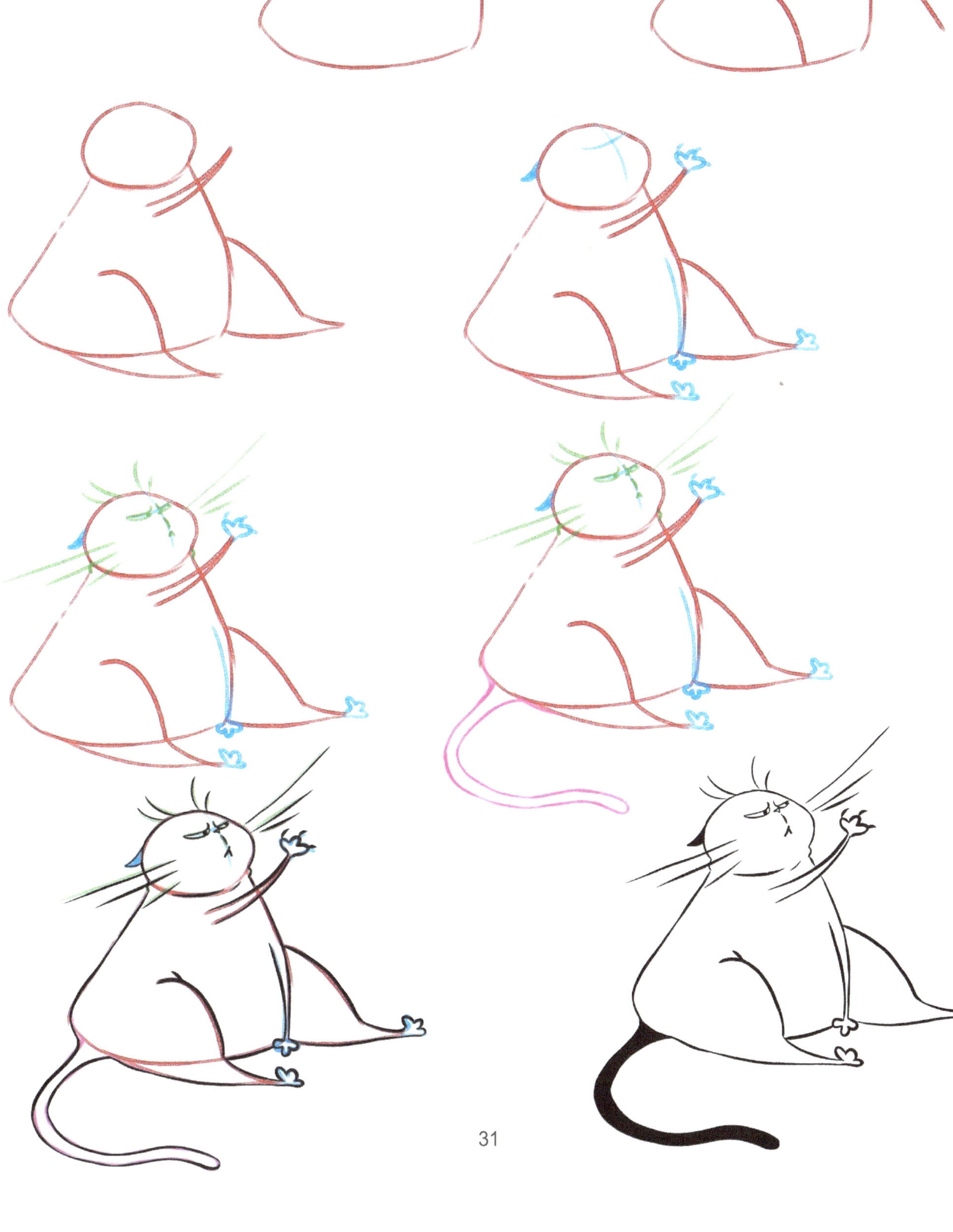

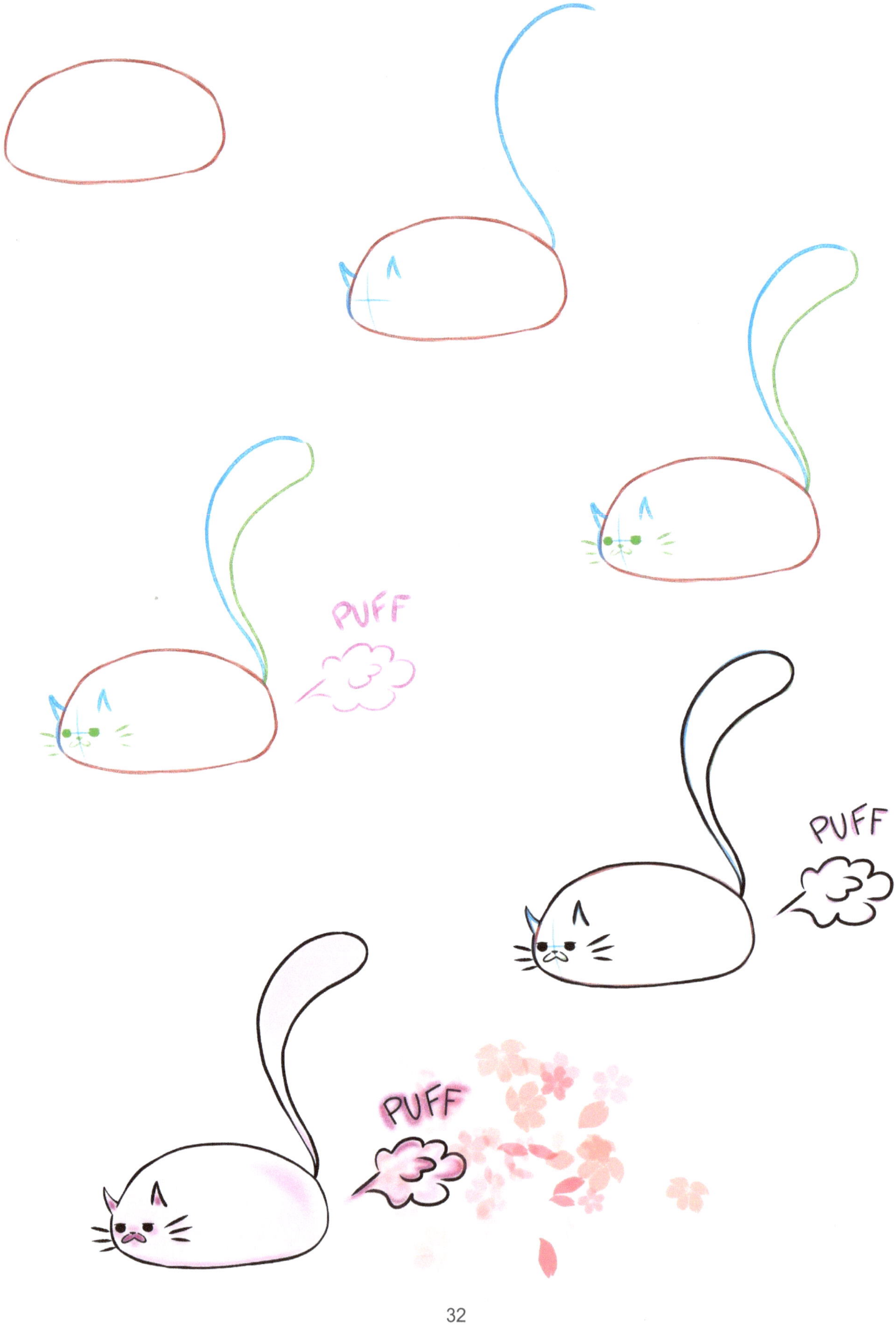
PUFF
PUFF
PUFF

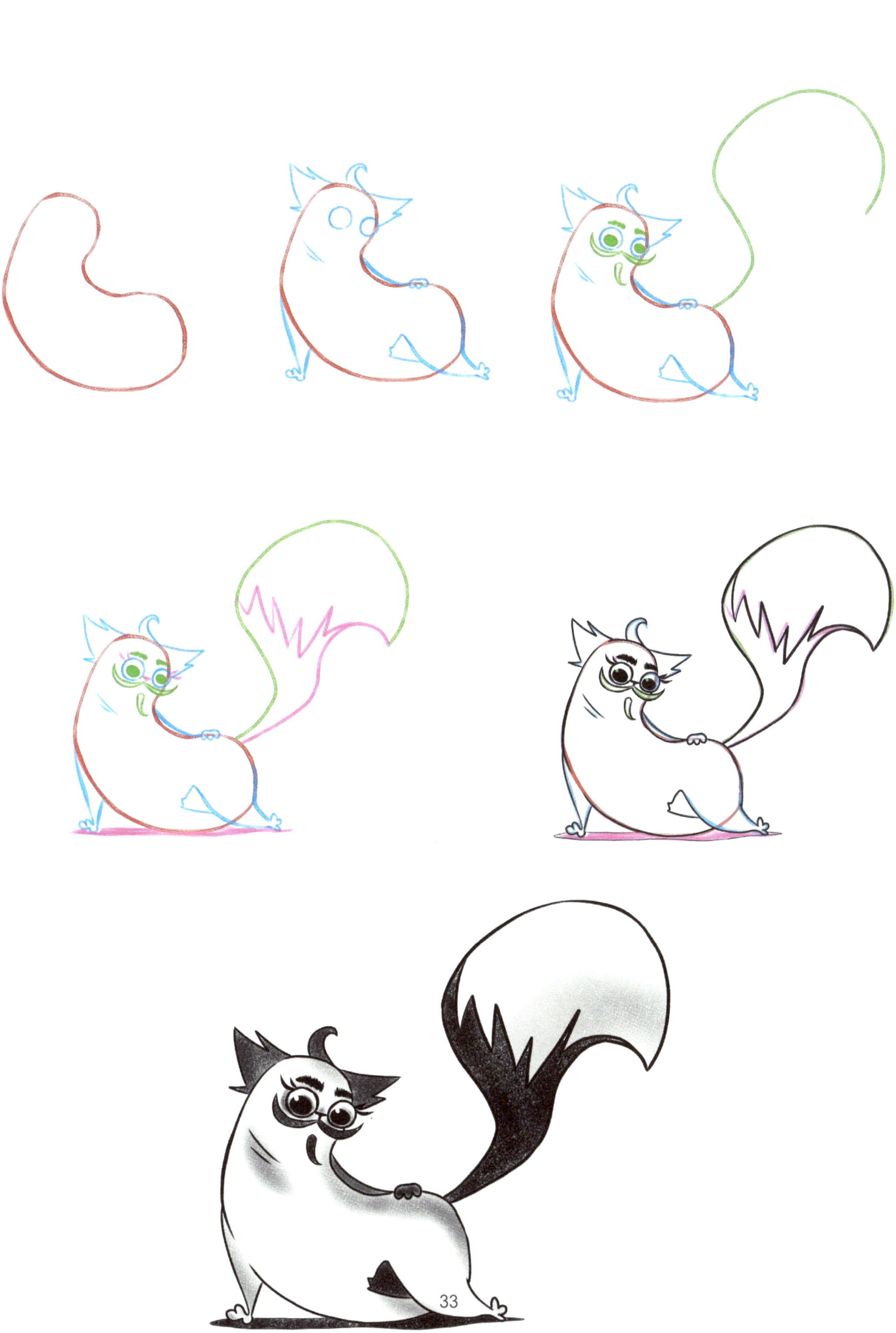

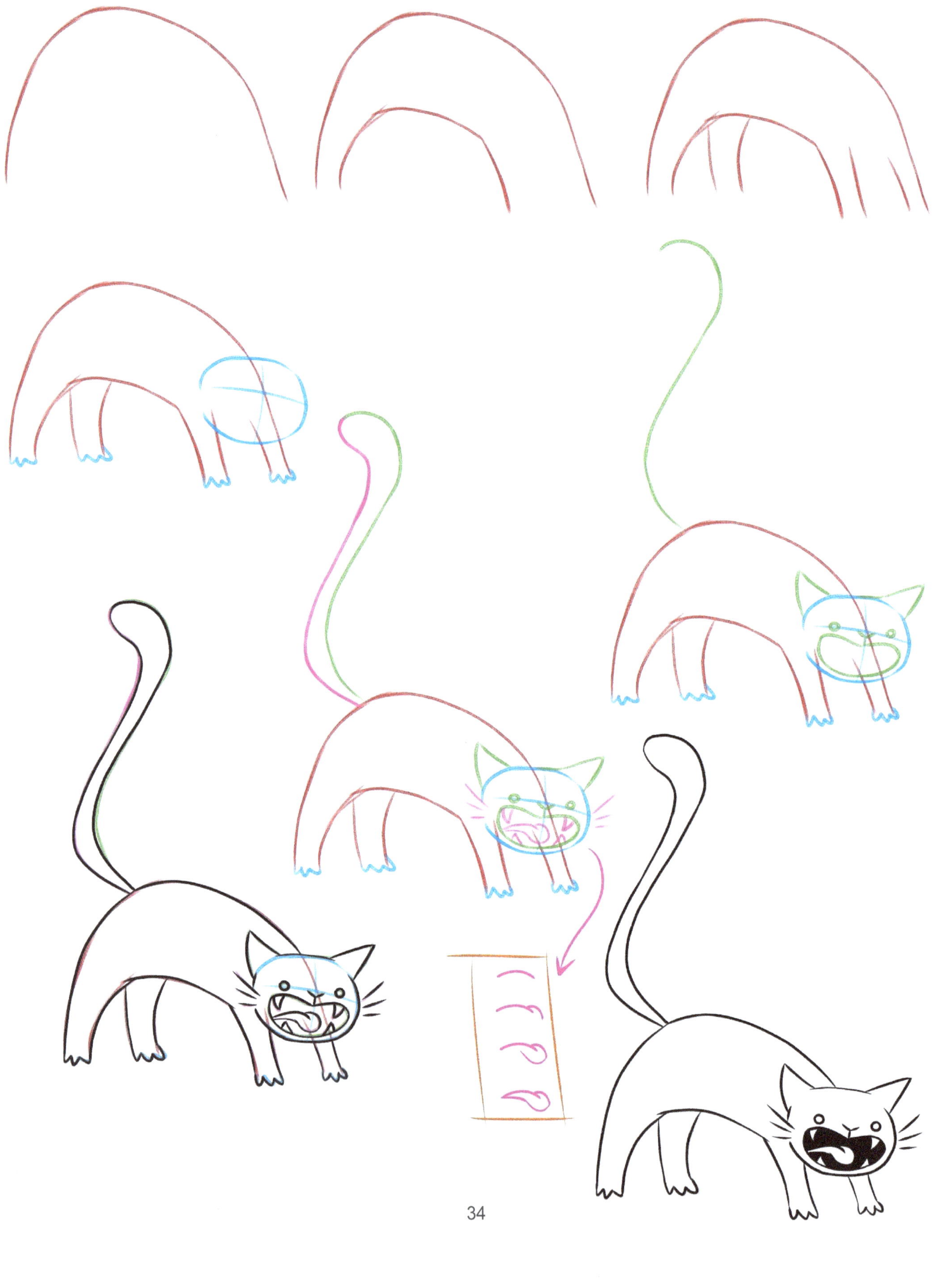

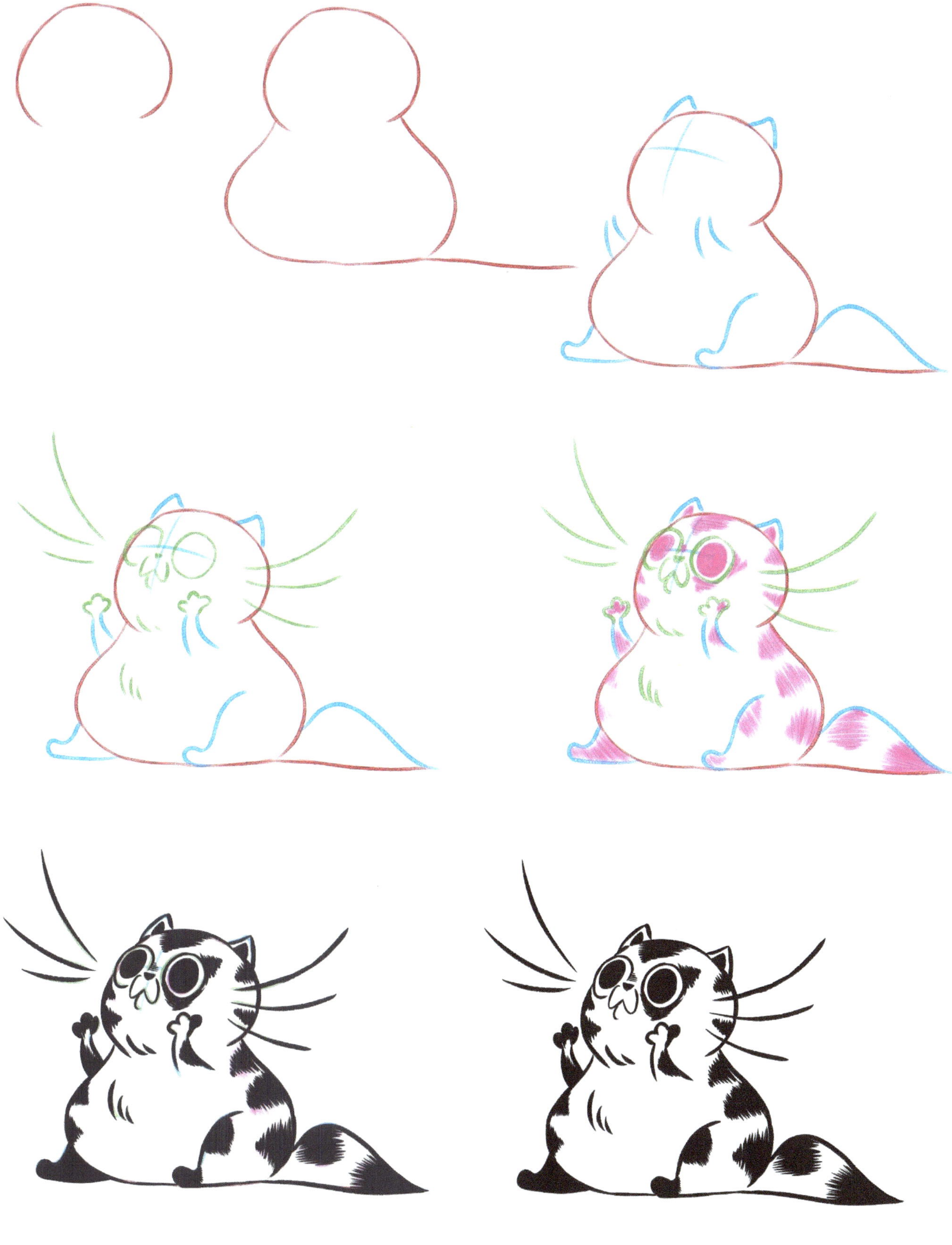

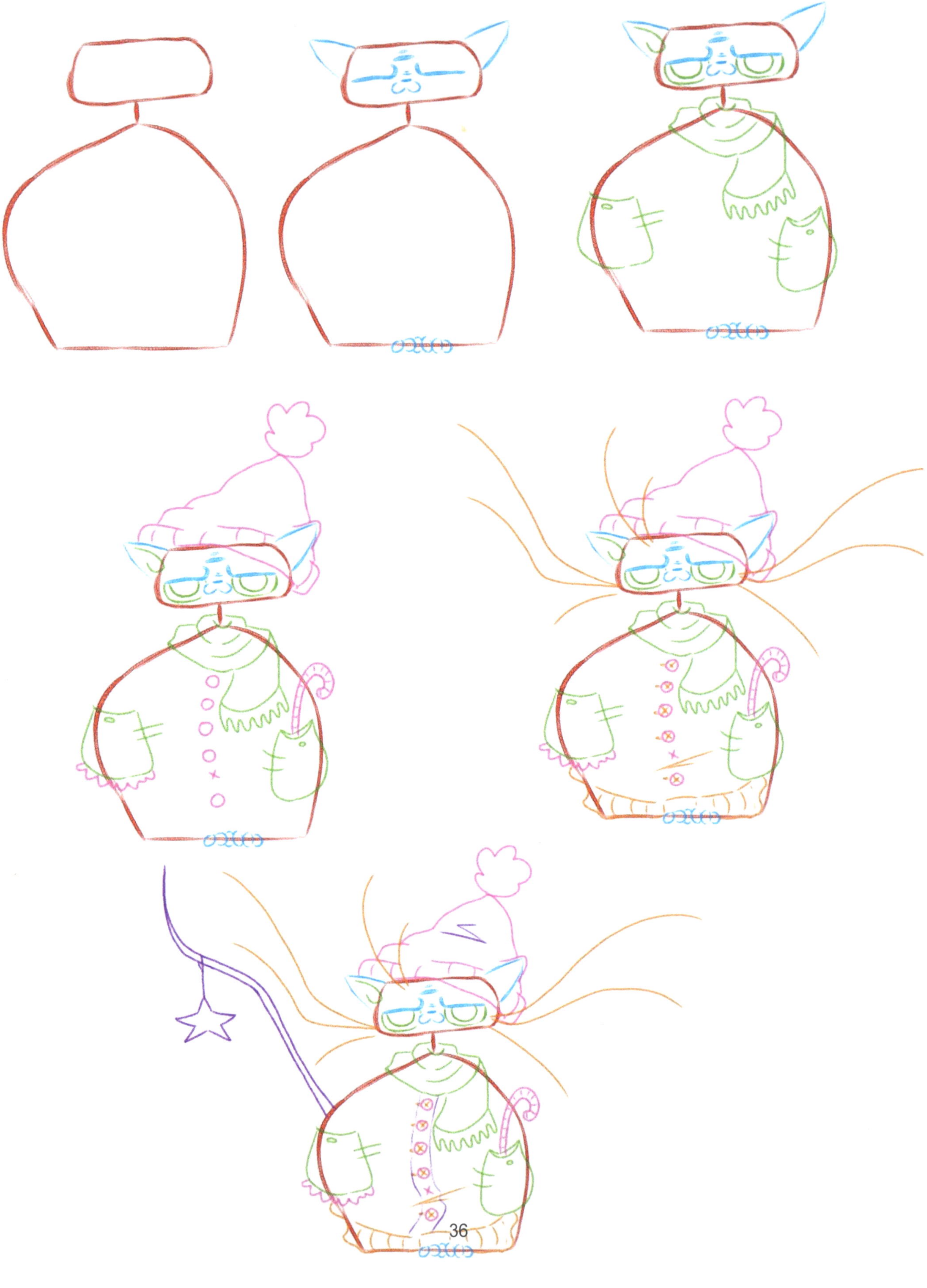

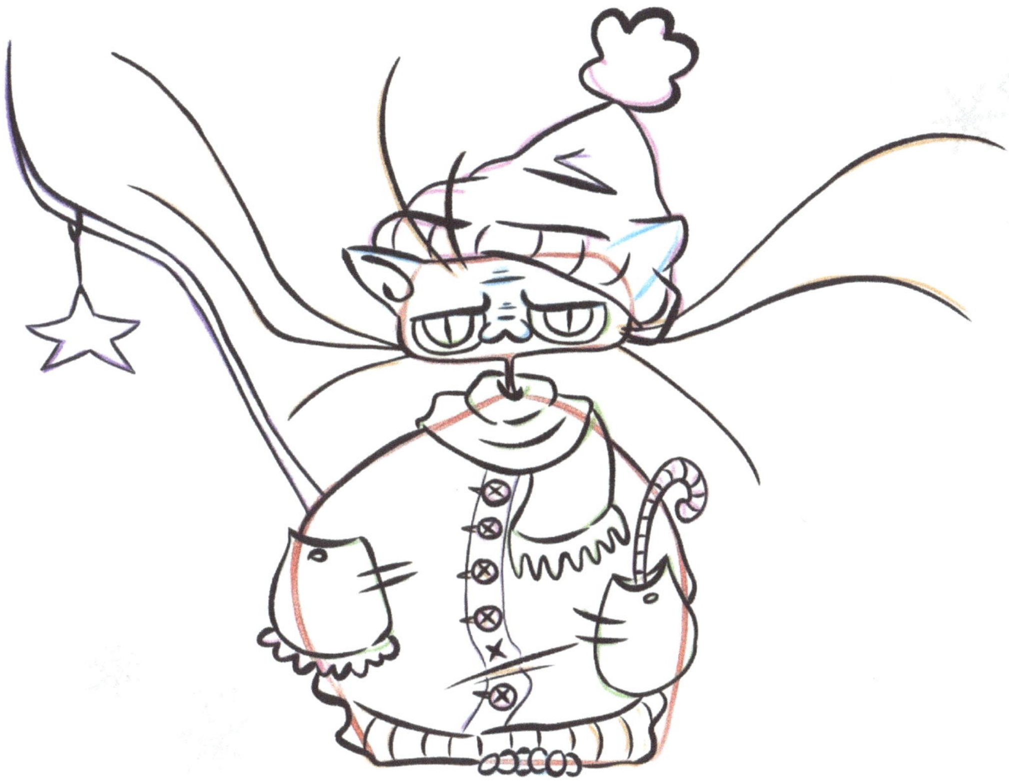

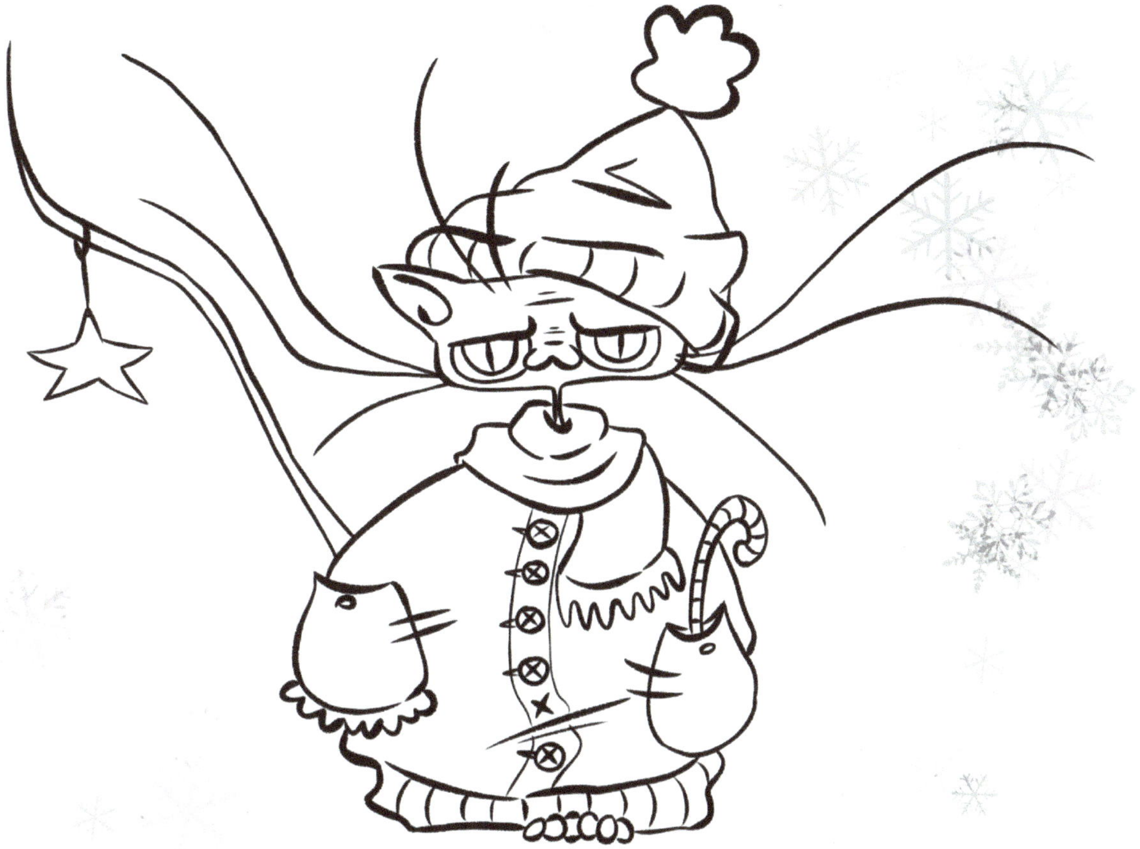

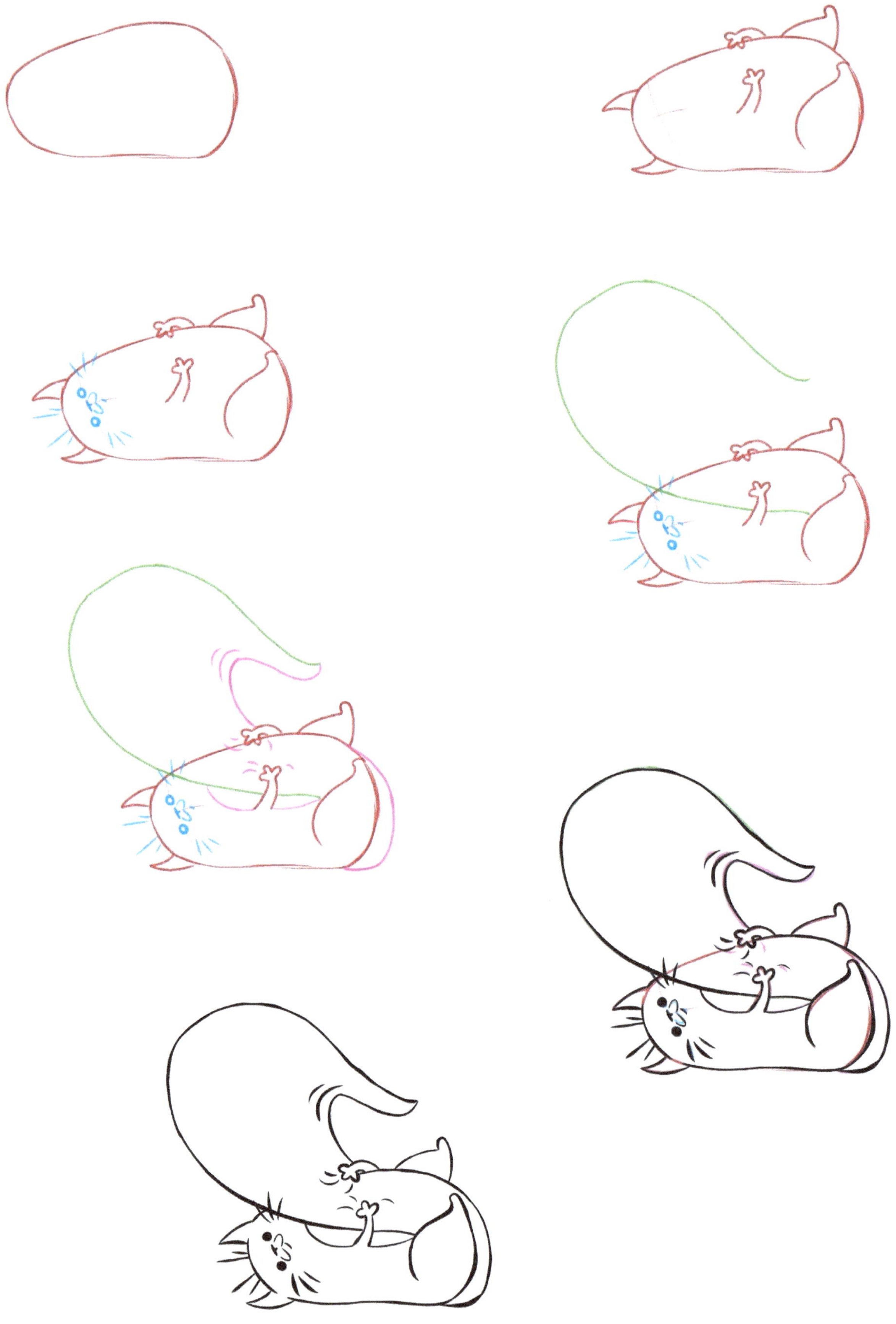

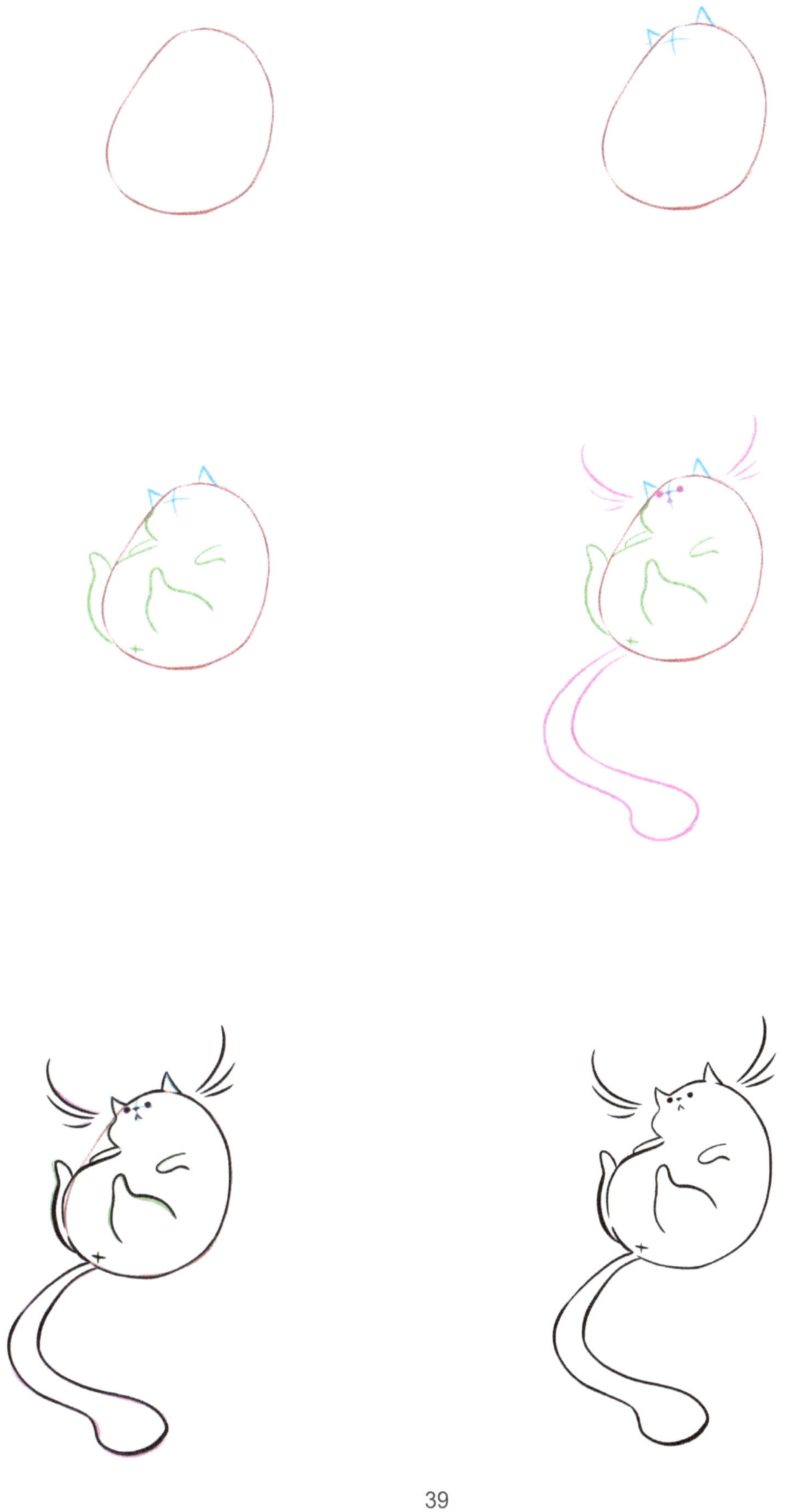

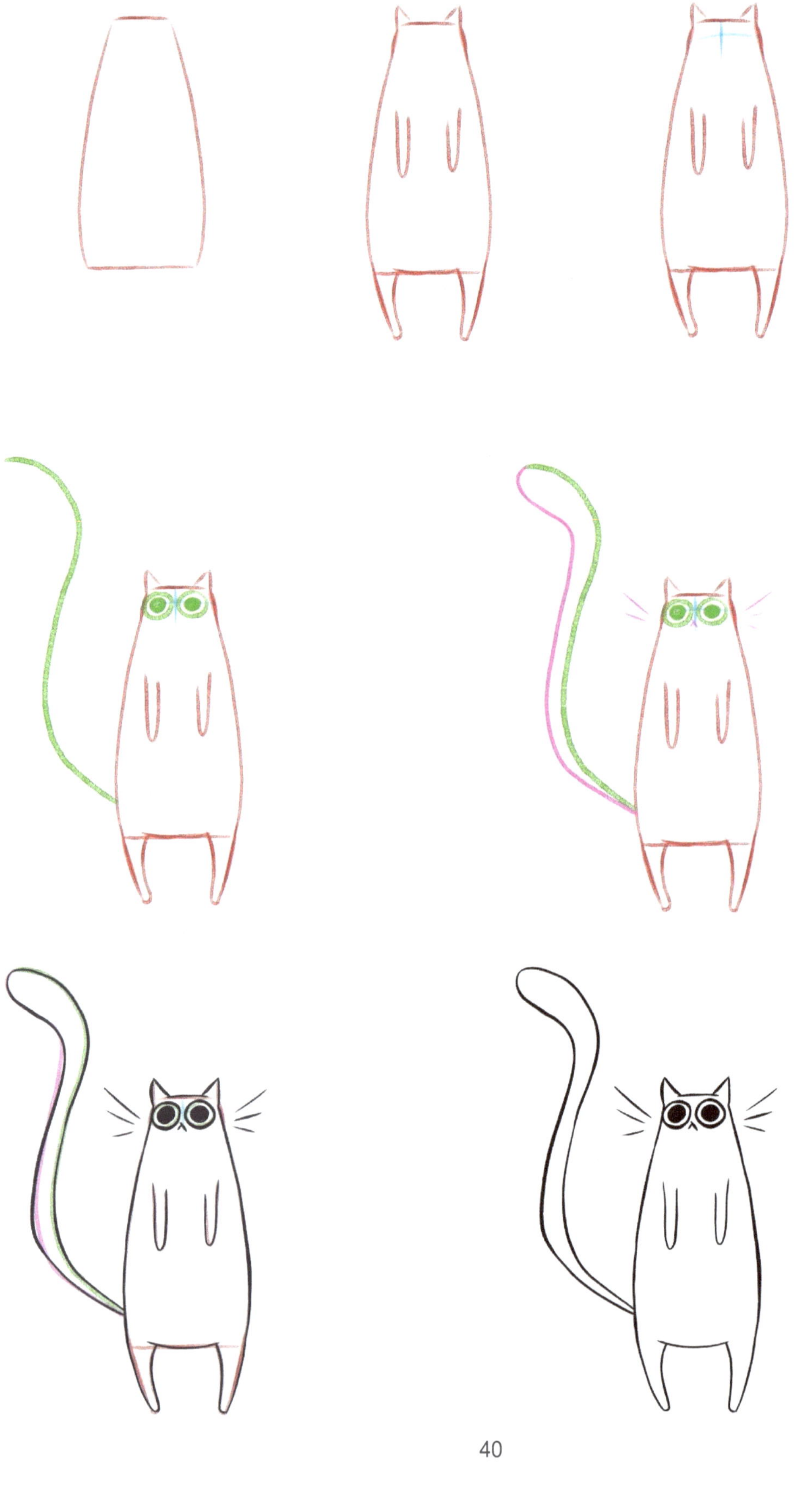

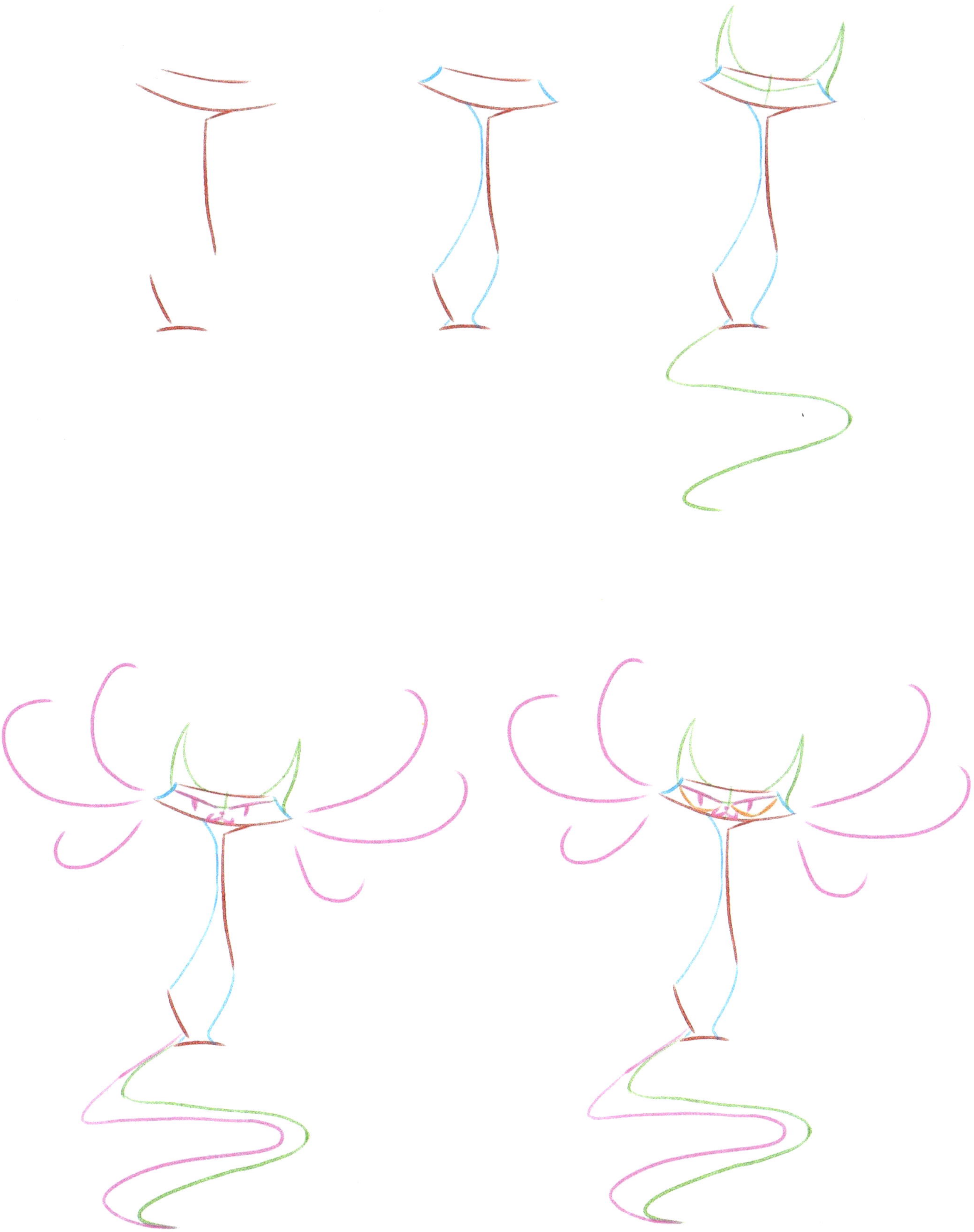

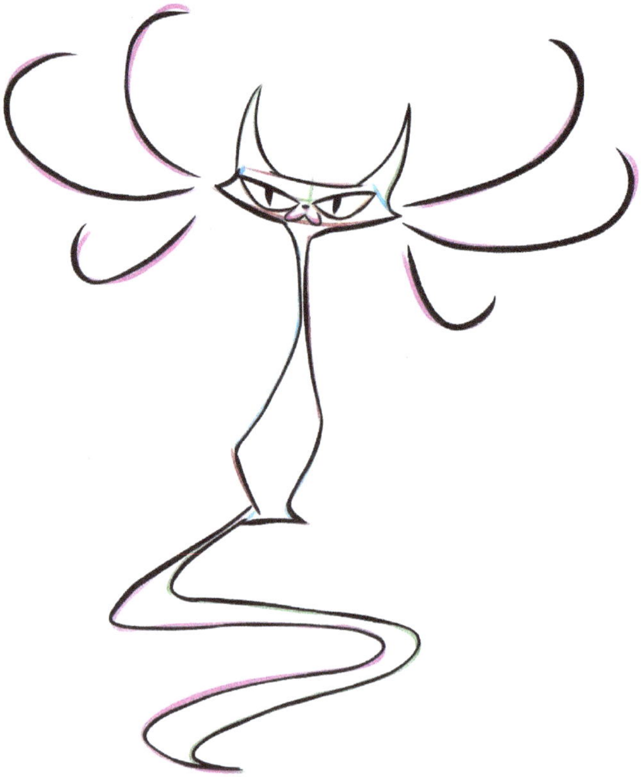

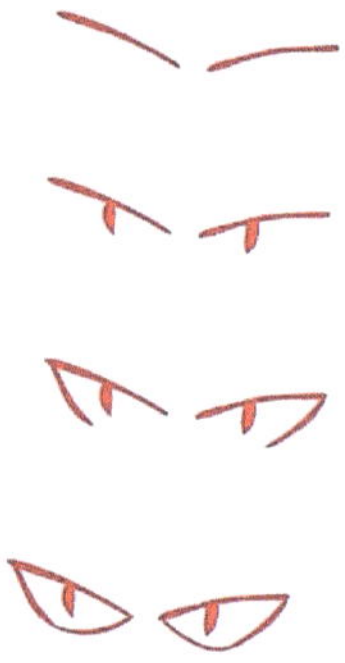

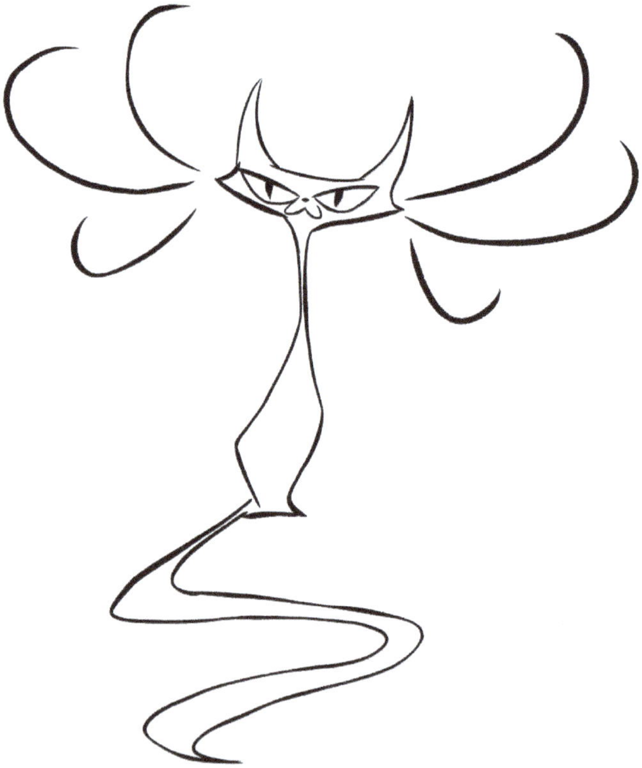

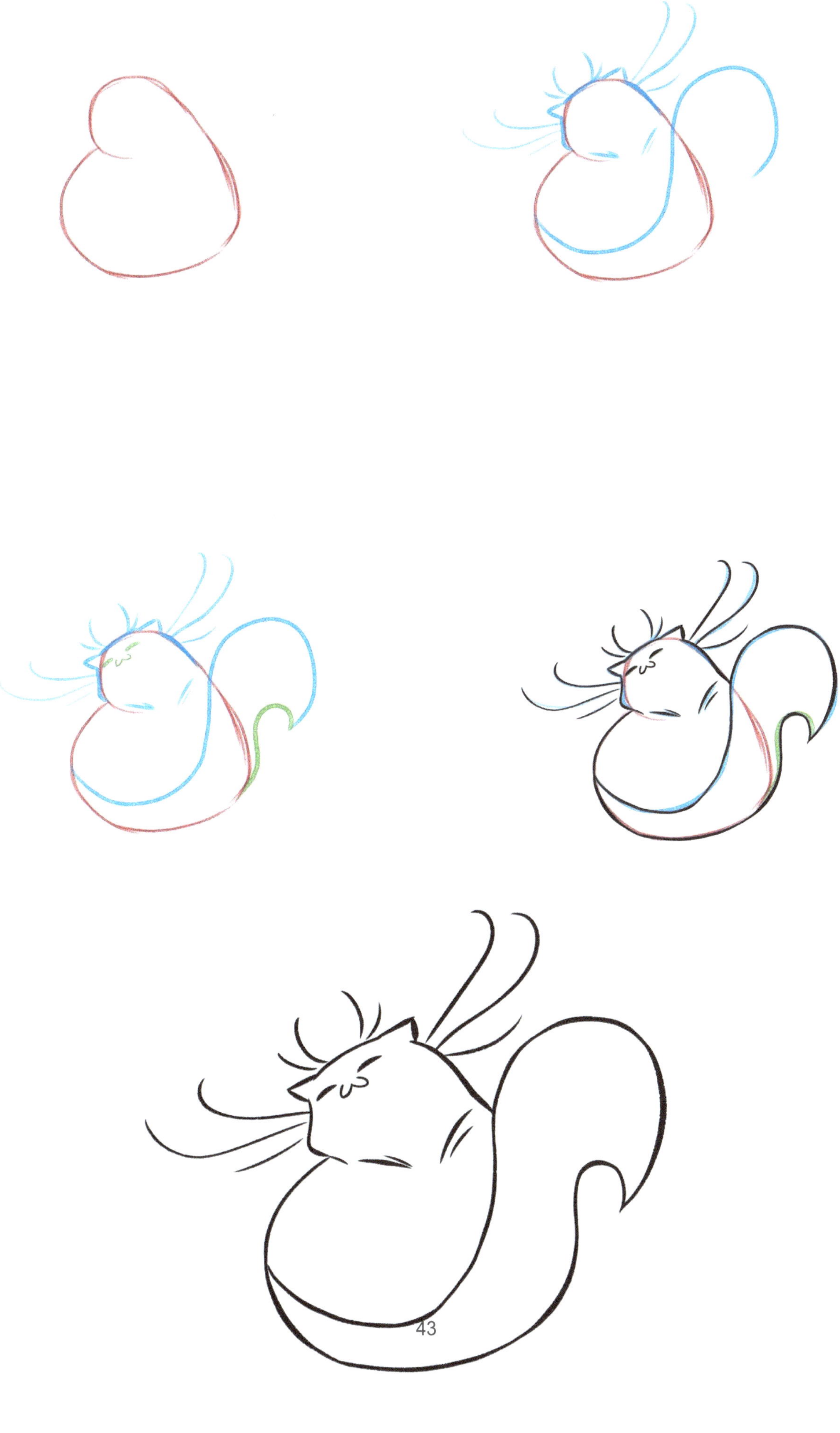

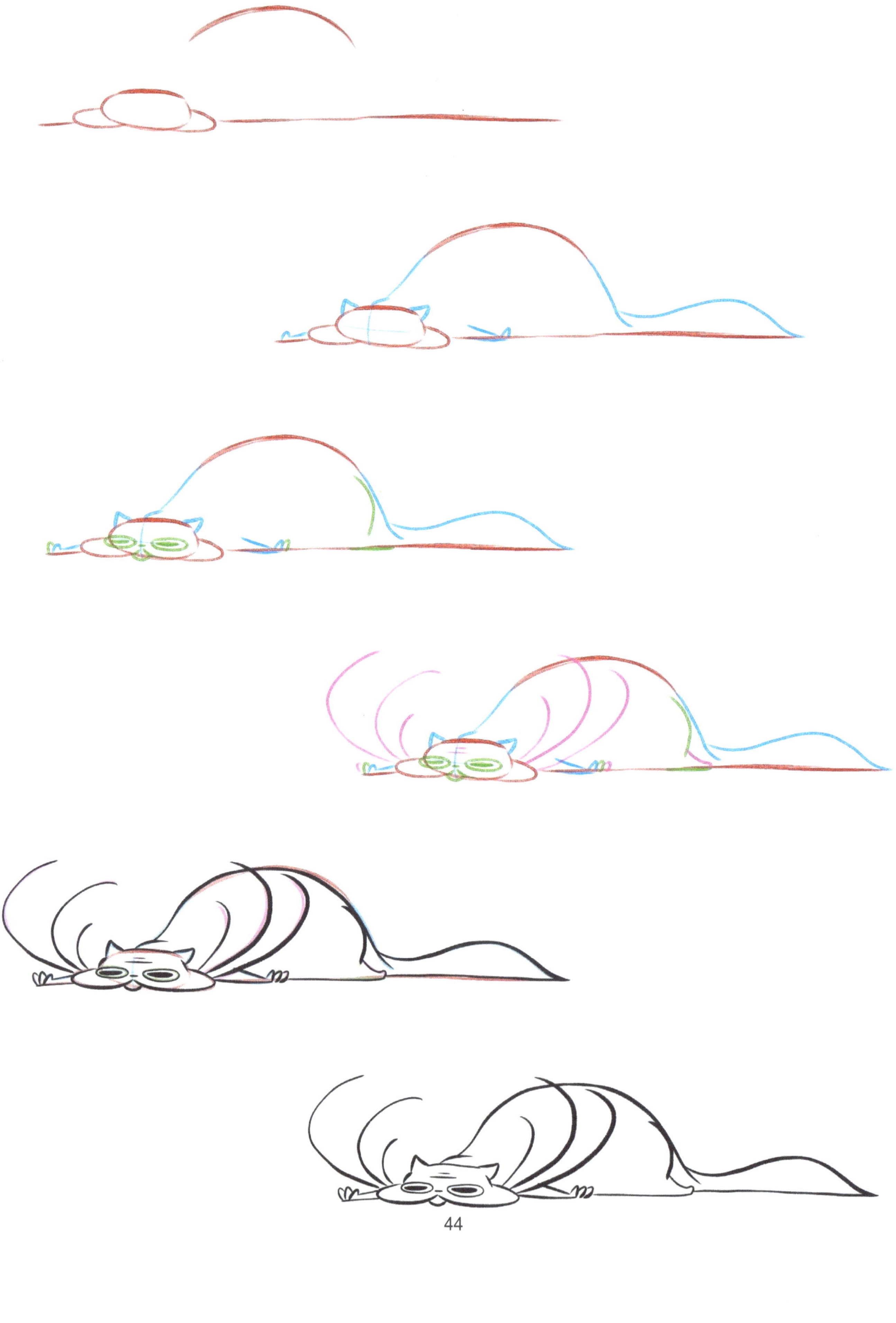

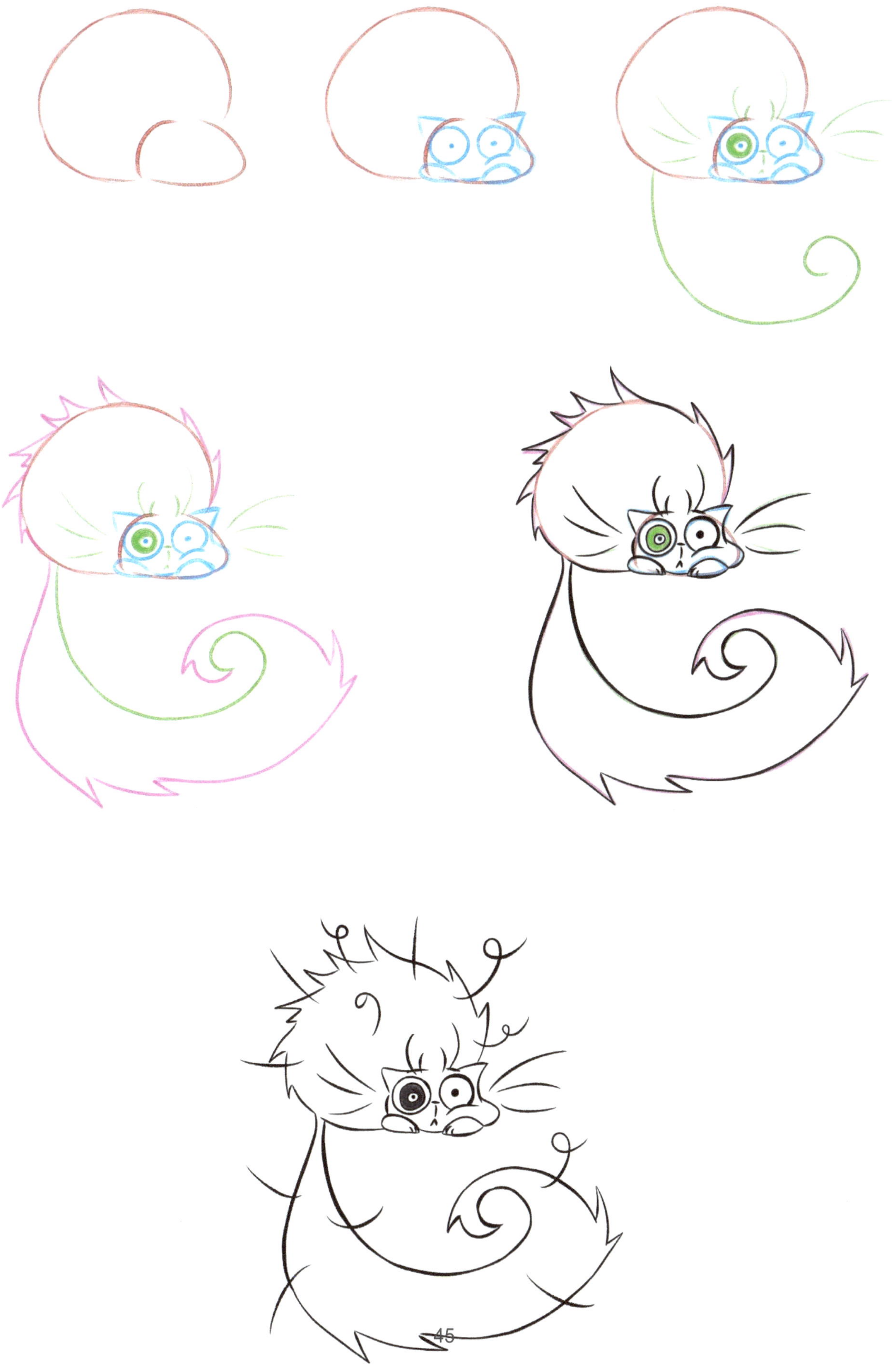

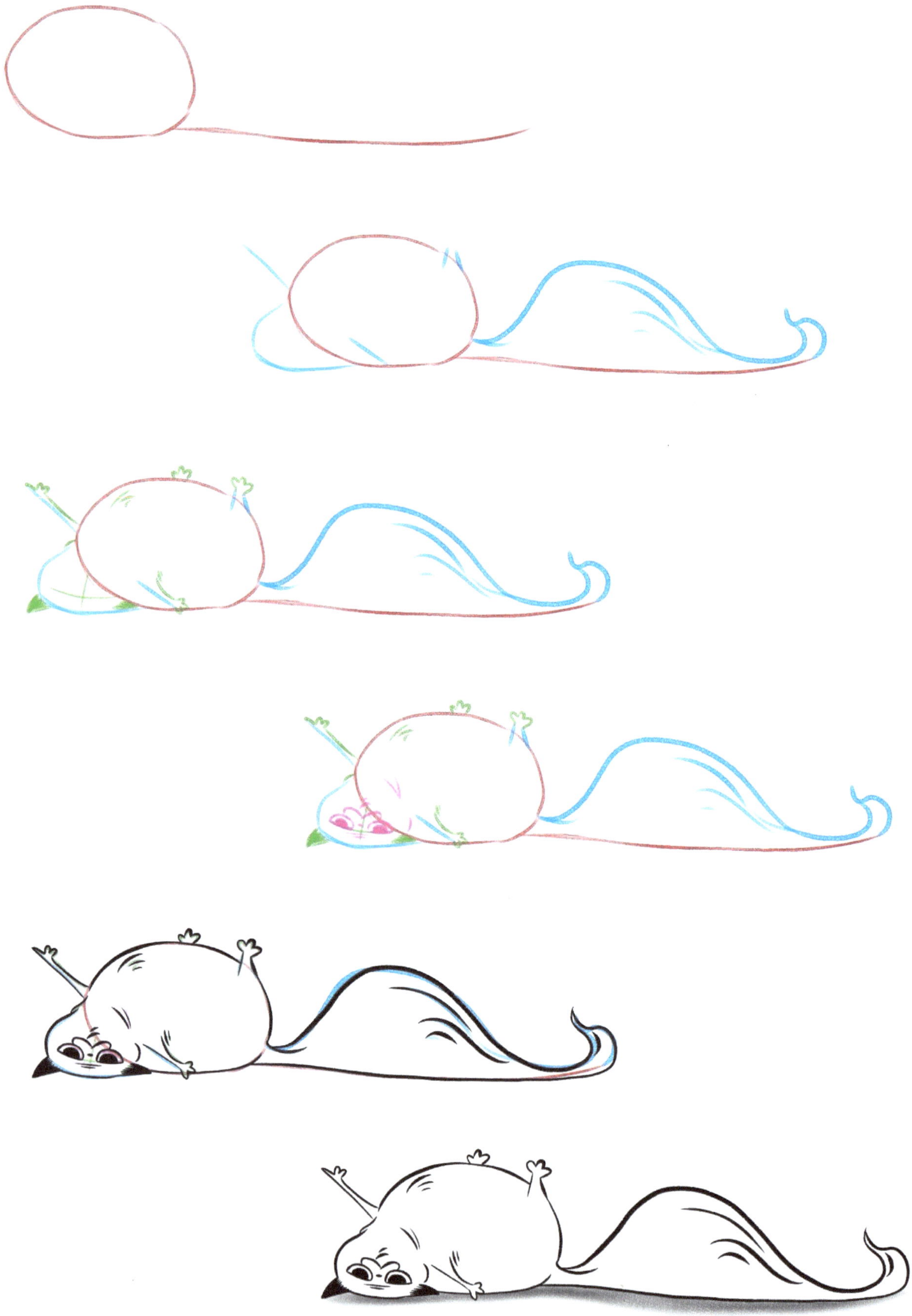

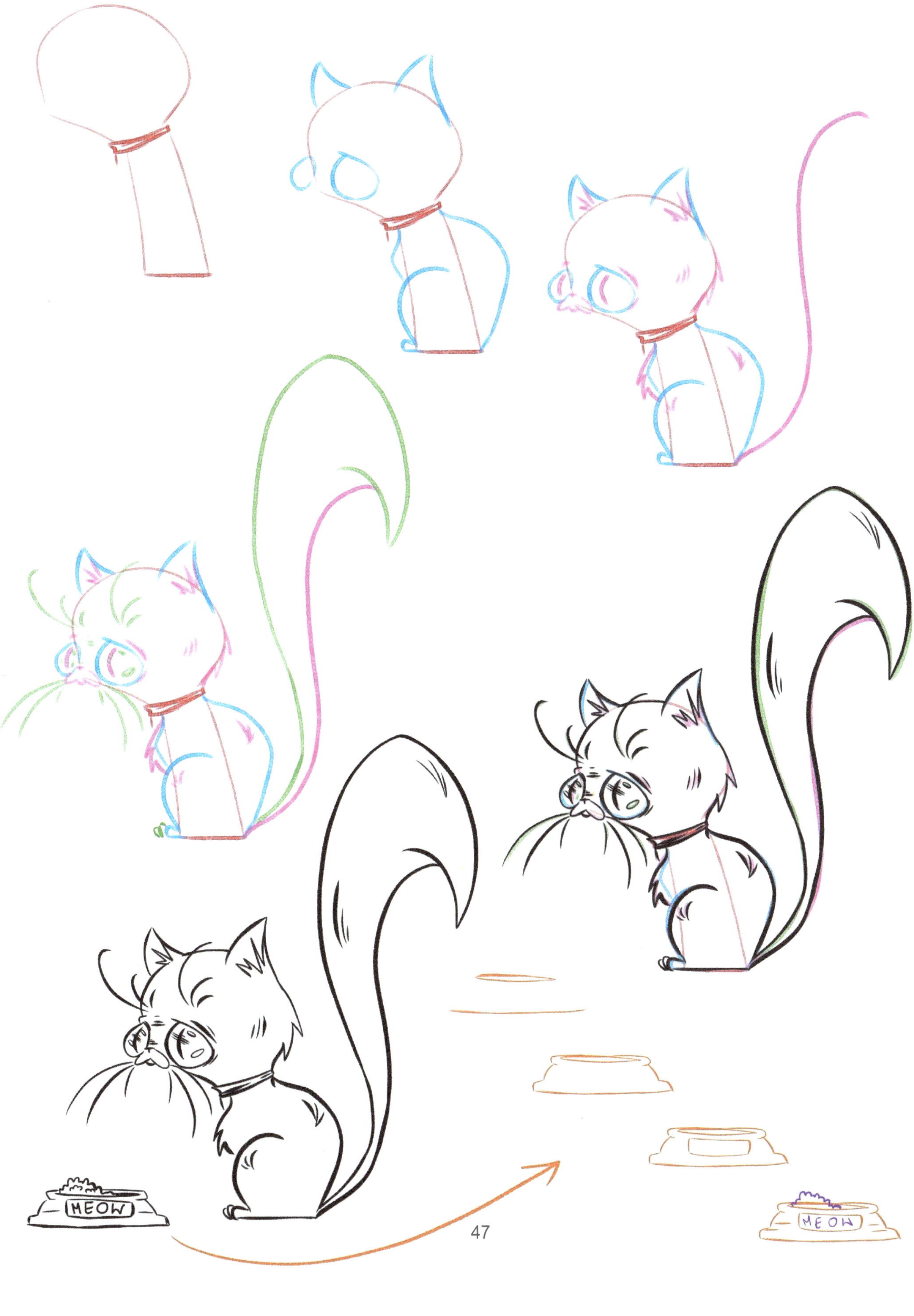
MEOW
MEOW

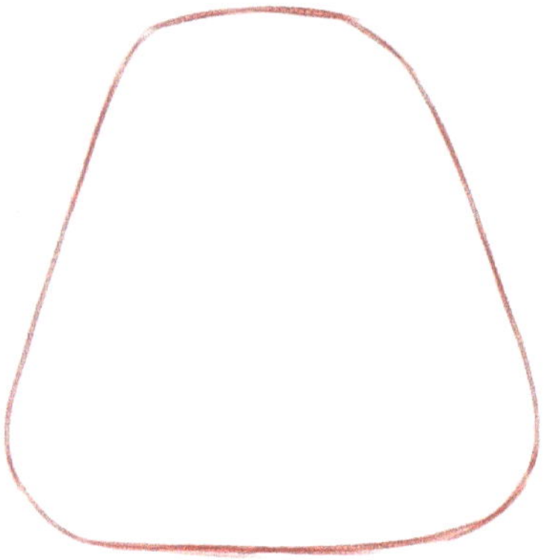

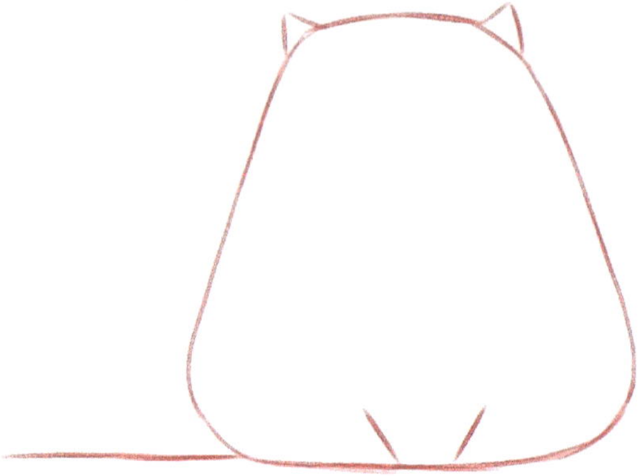

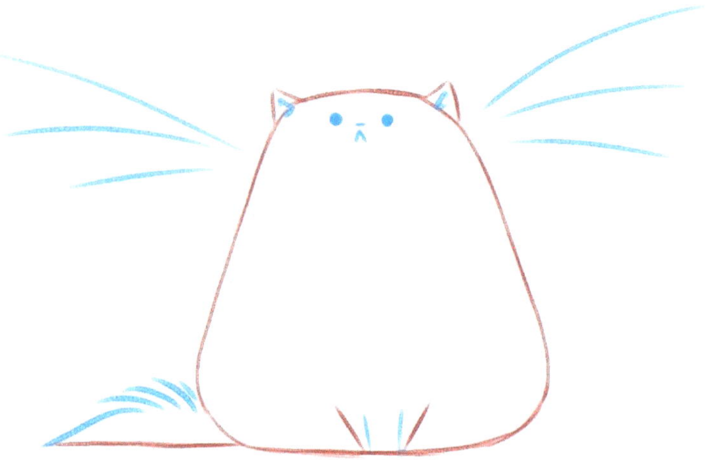

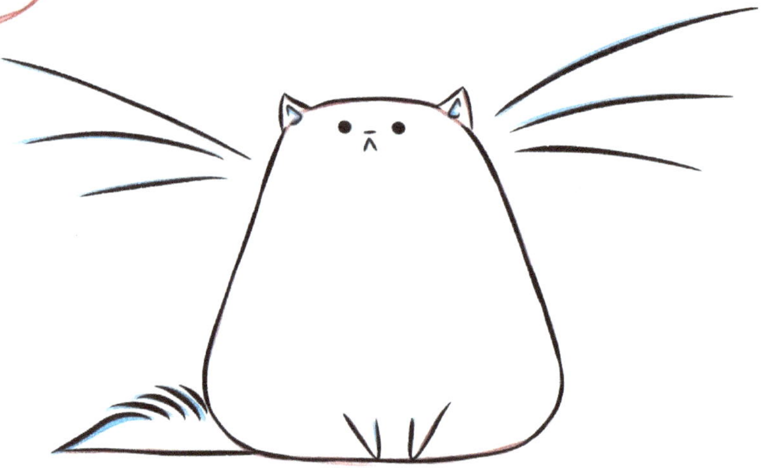

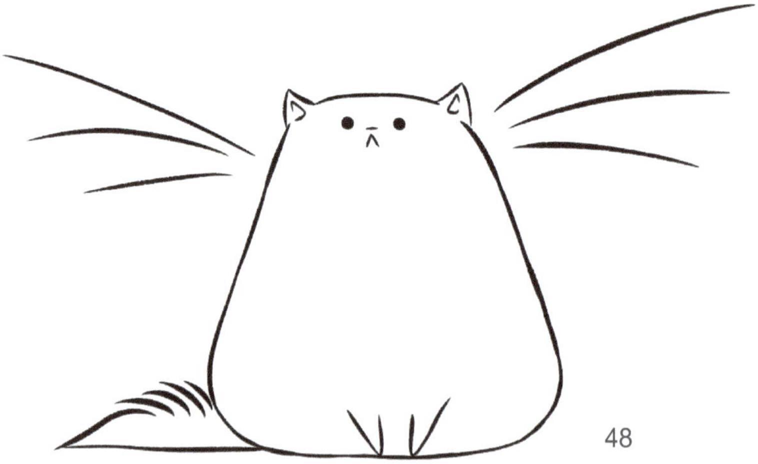

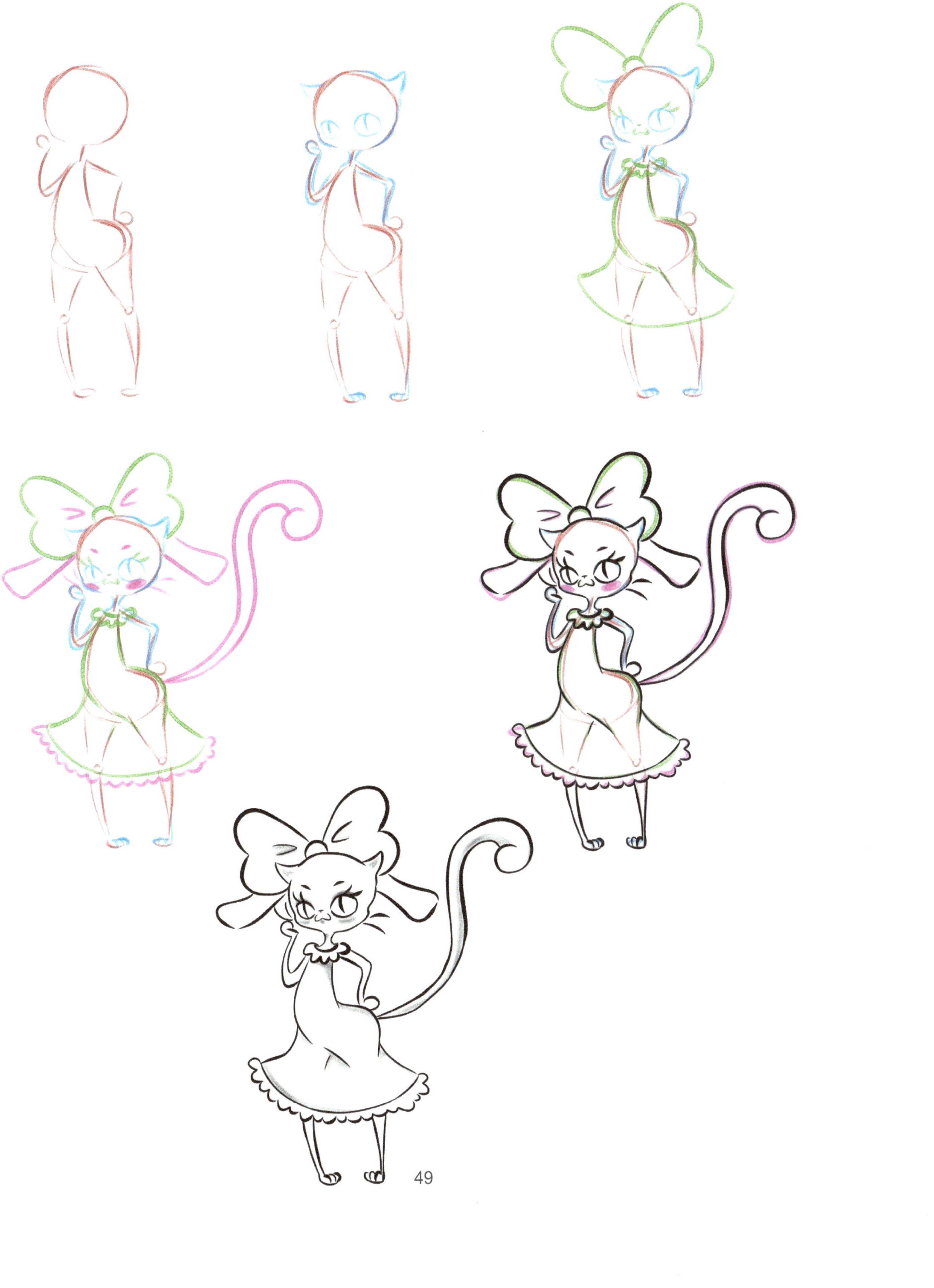

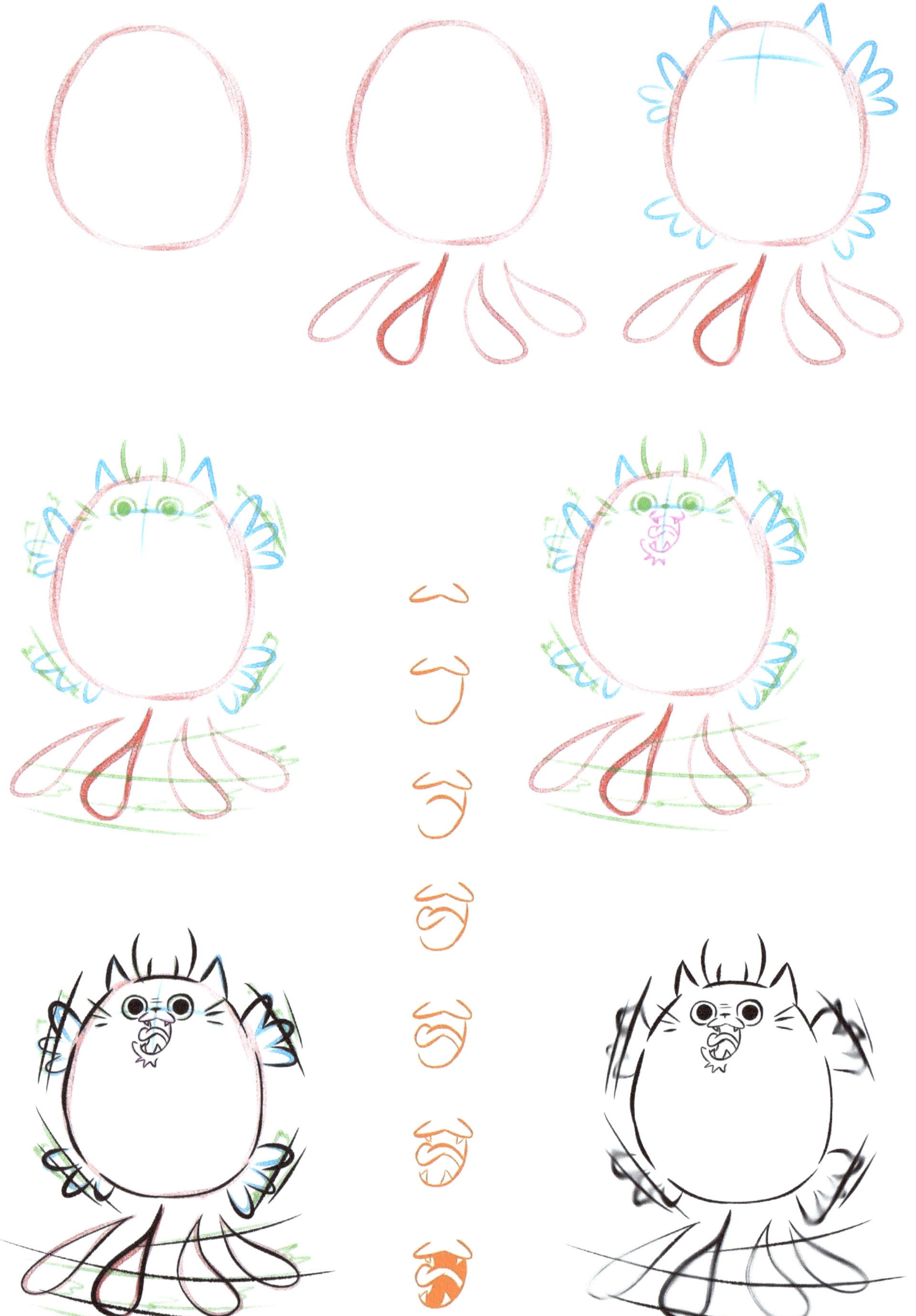

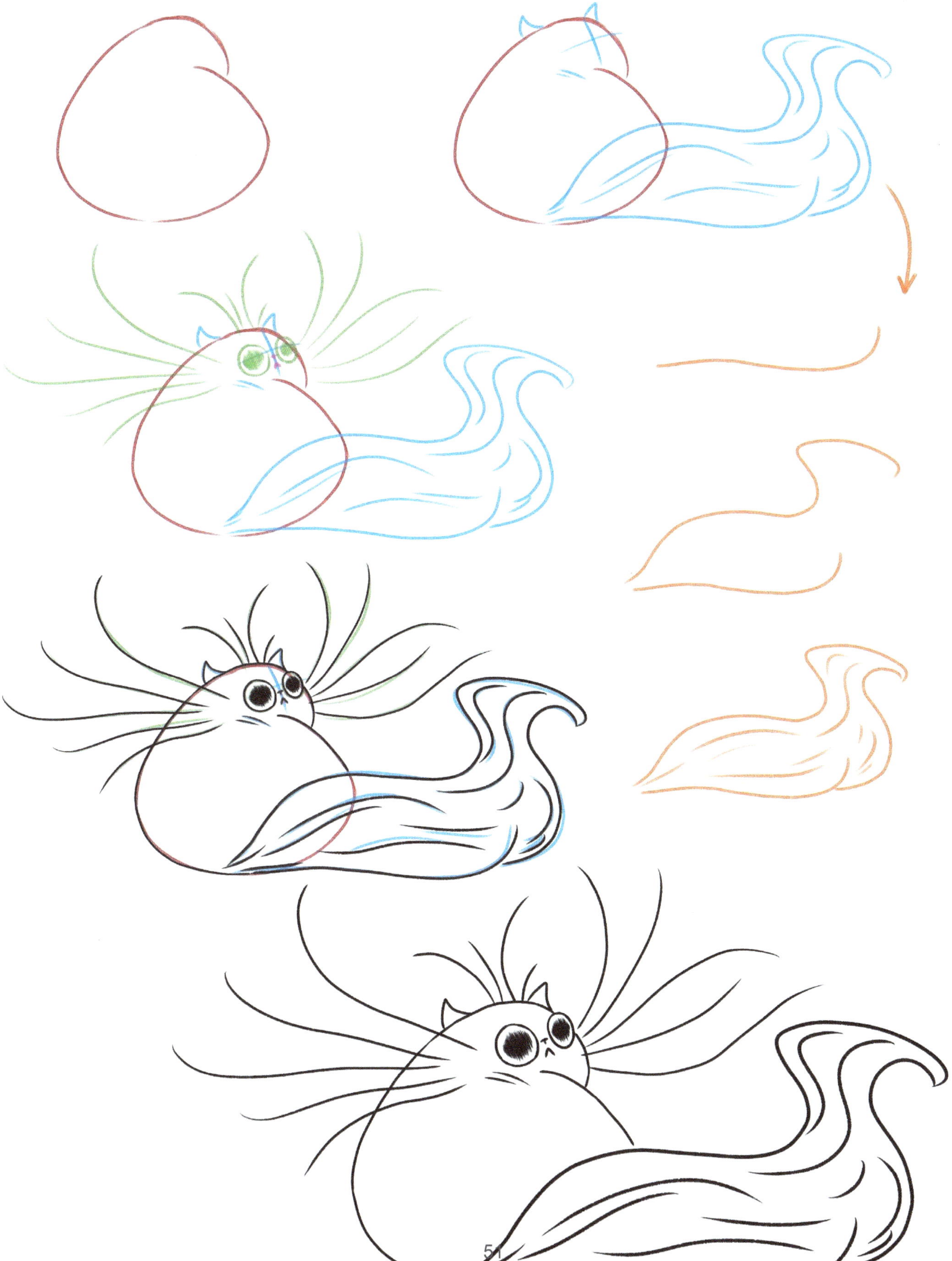

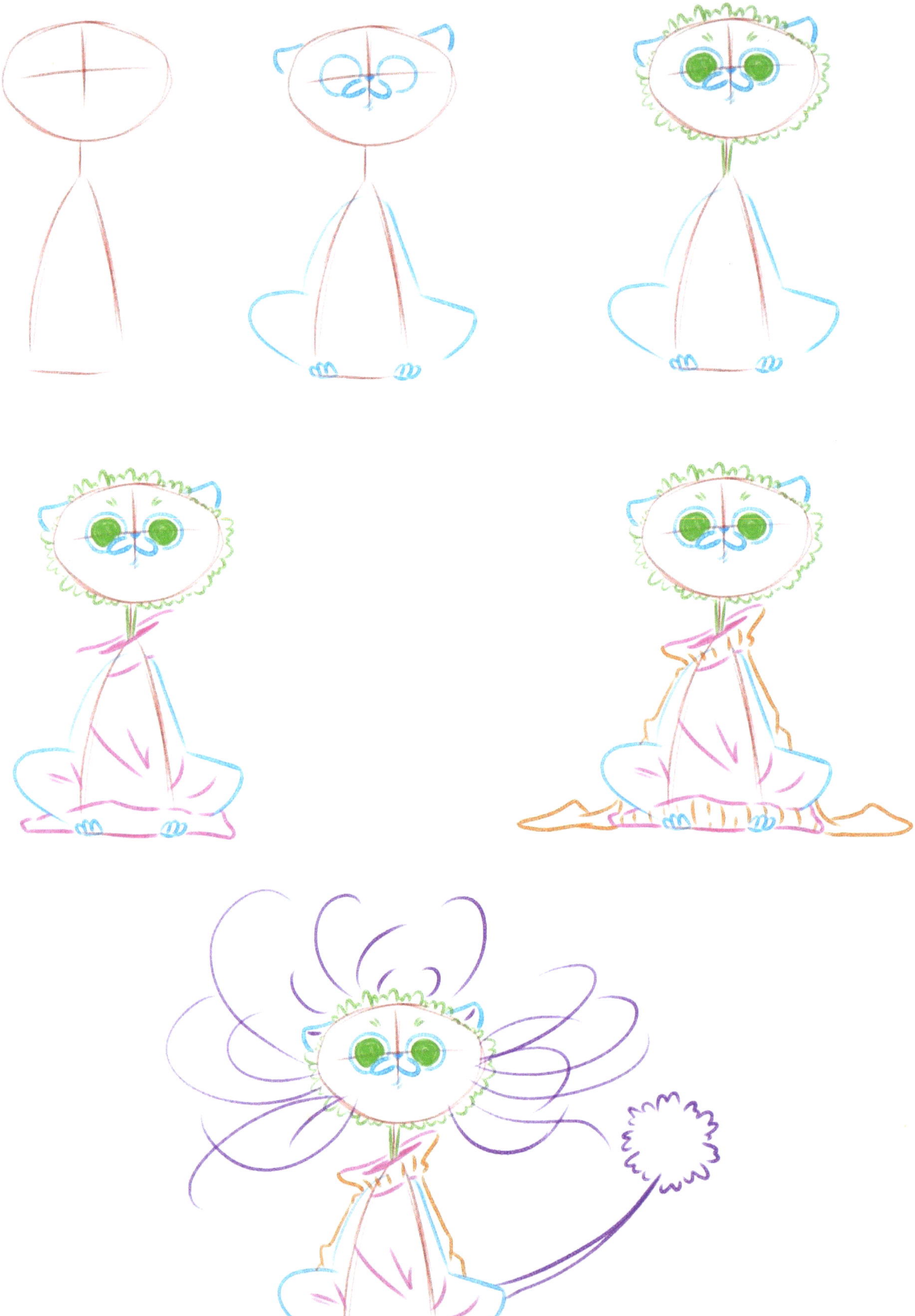

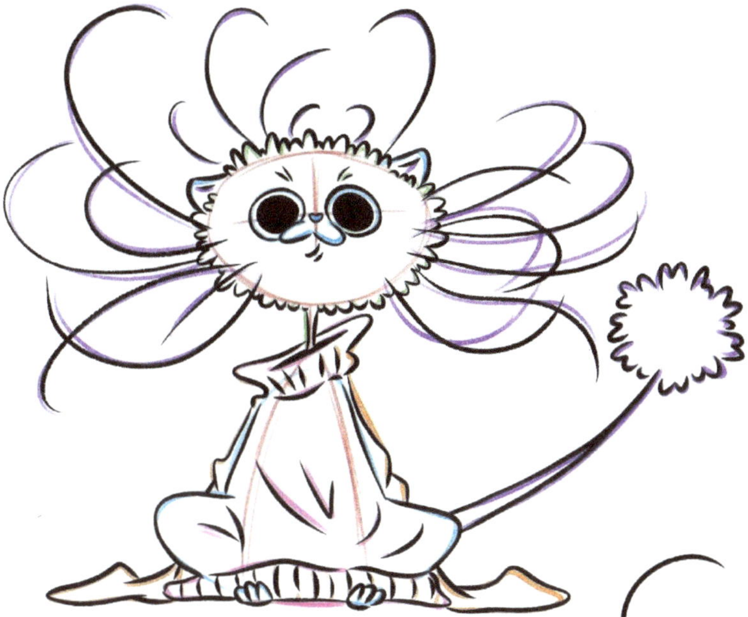

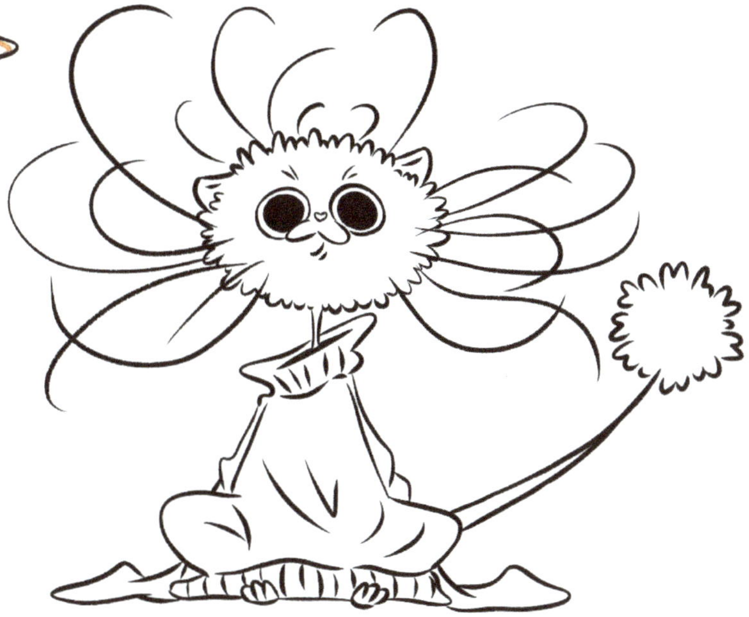

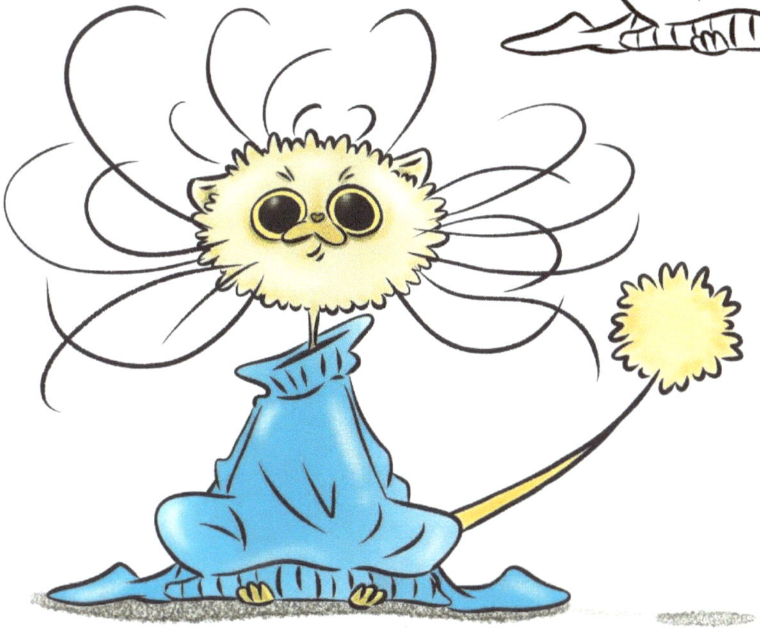

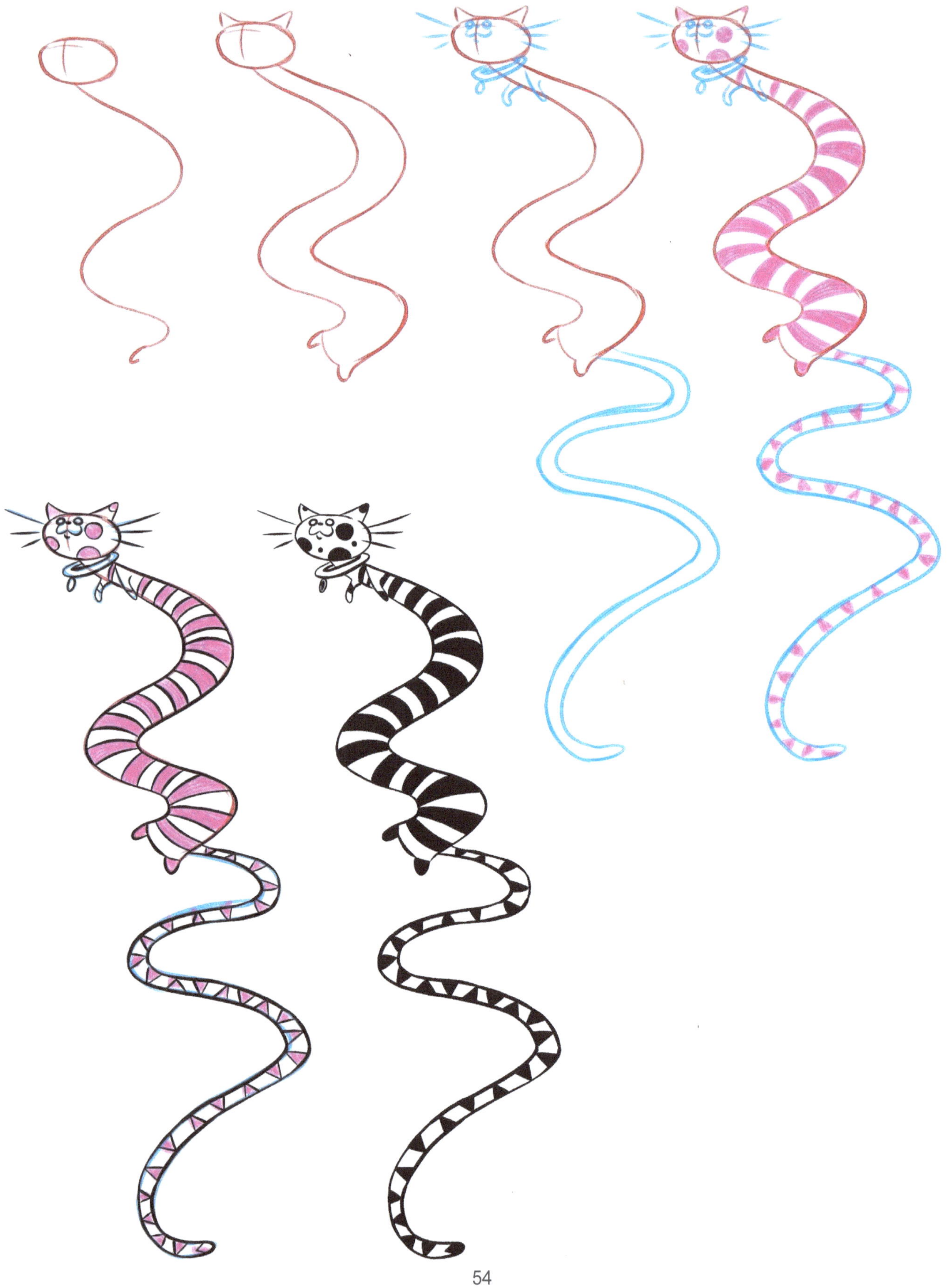

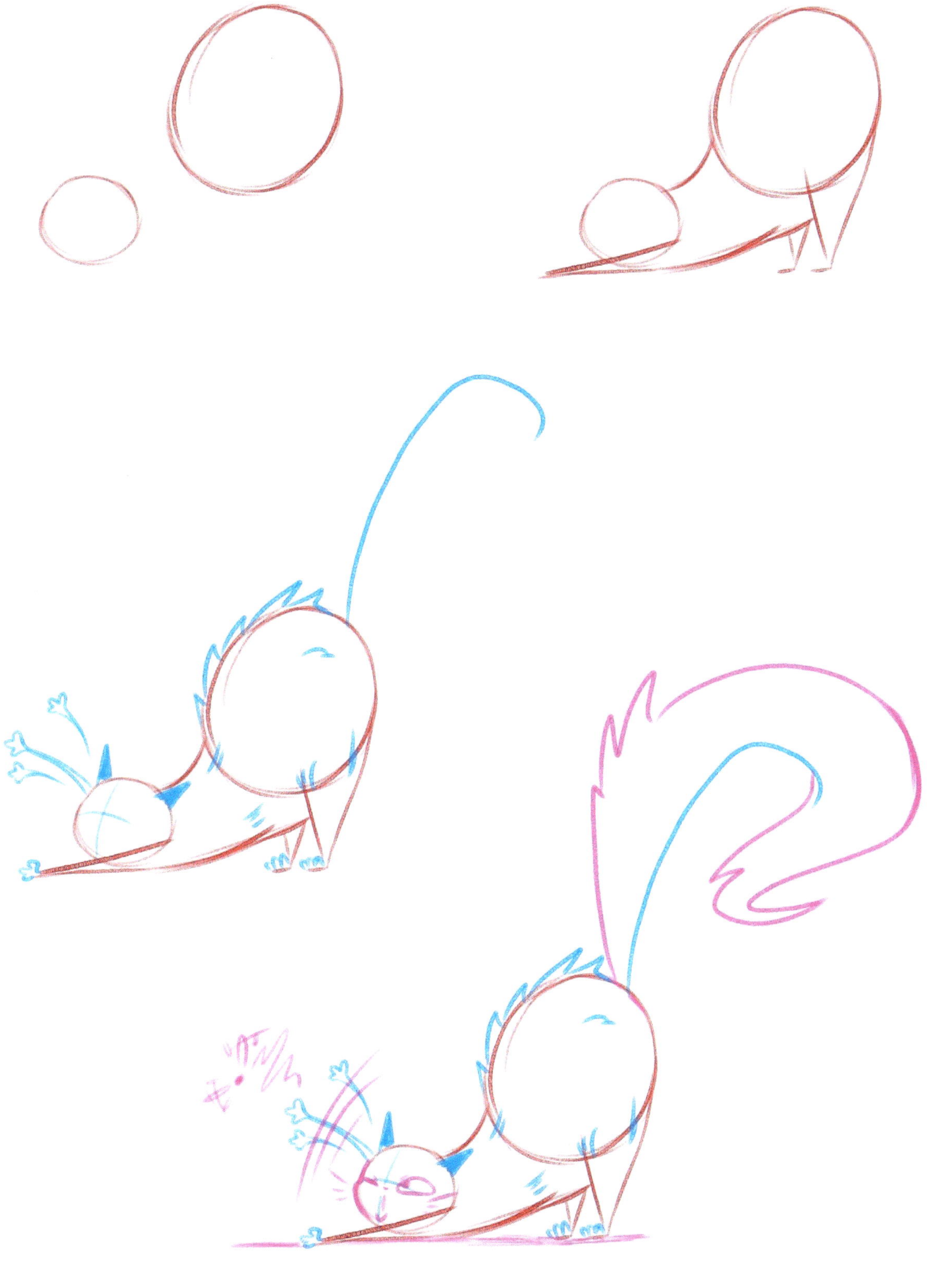

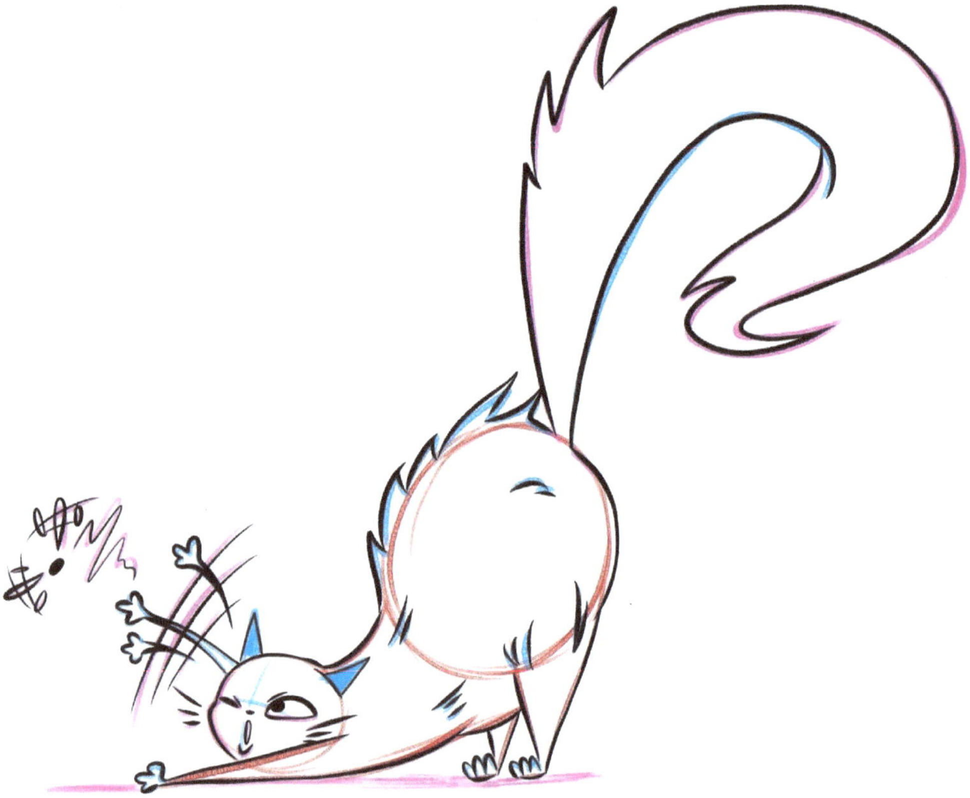

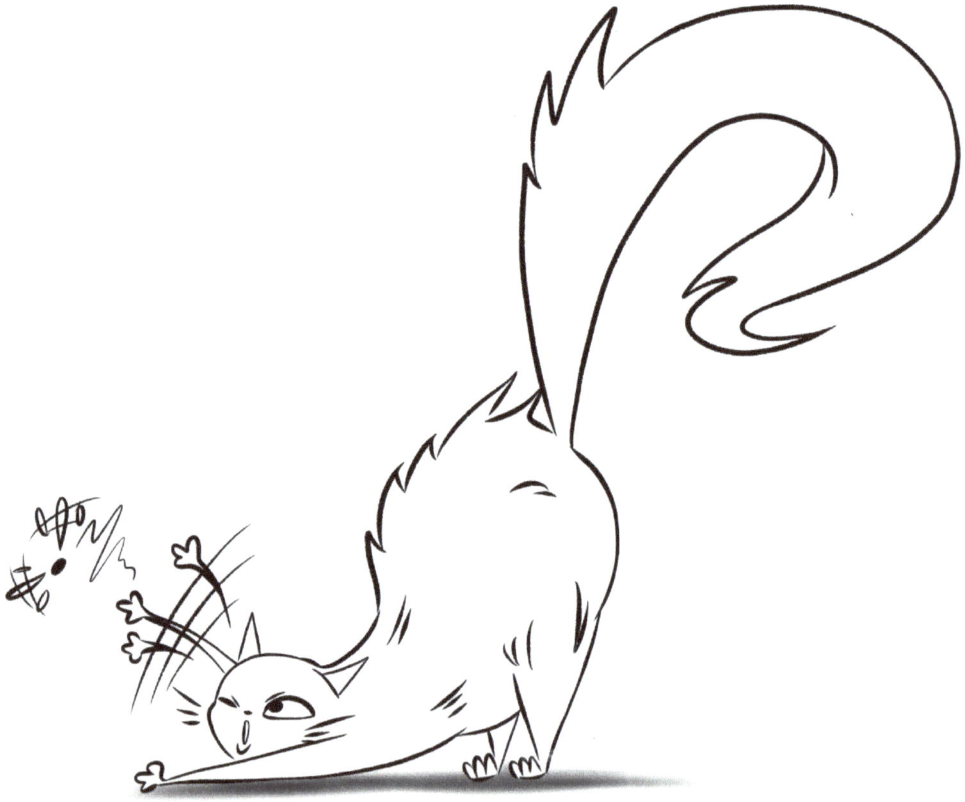

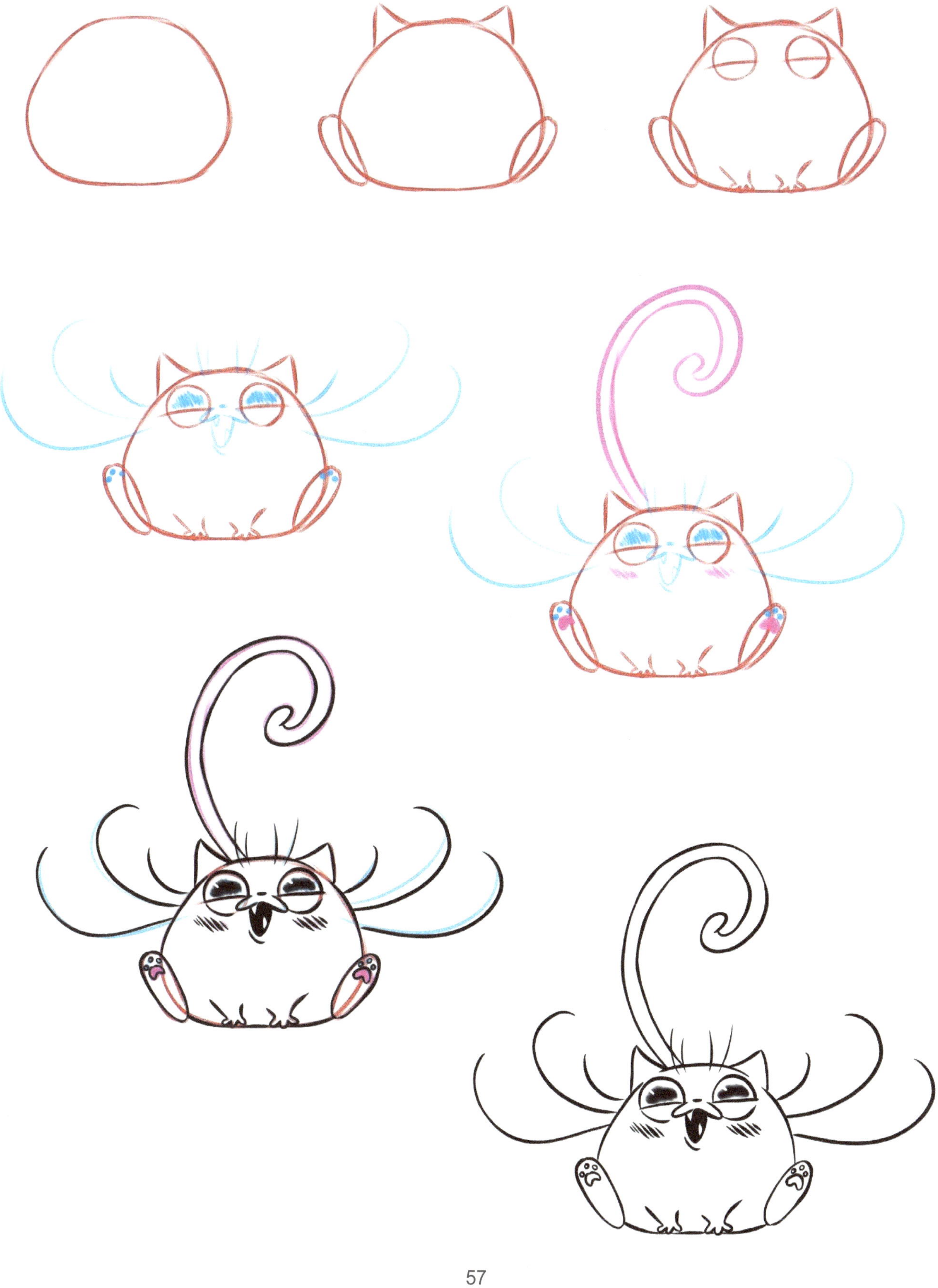

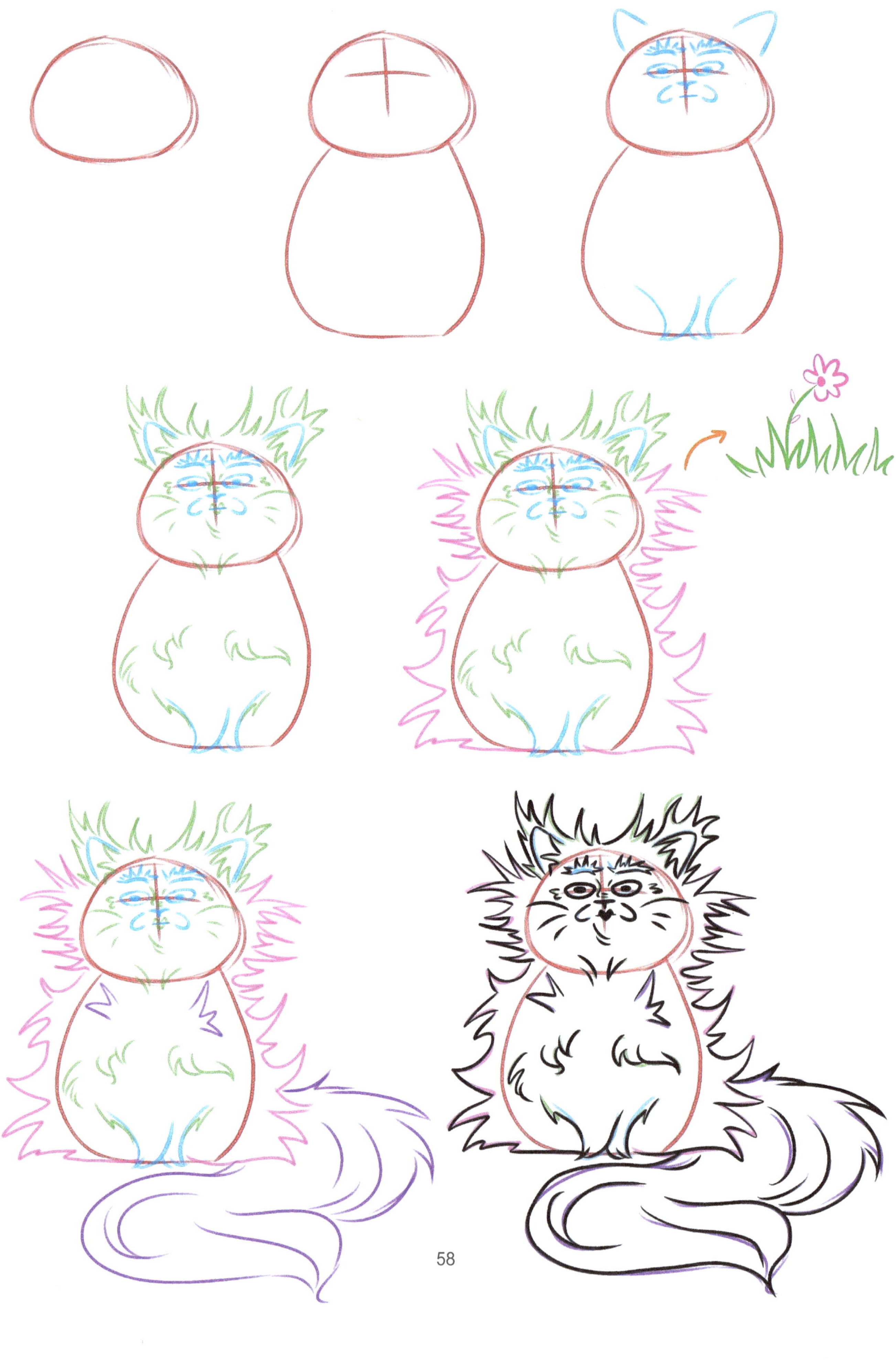

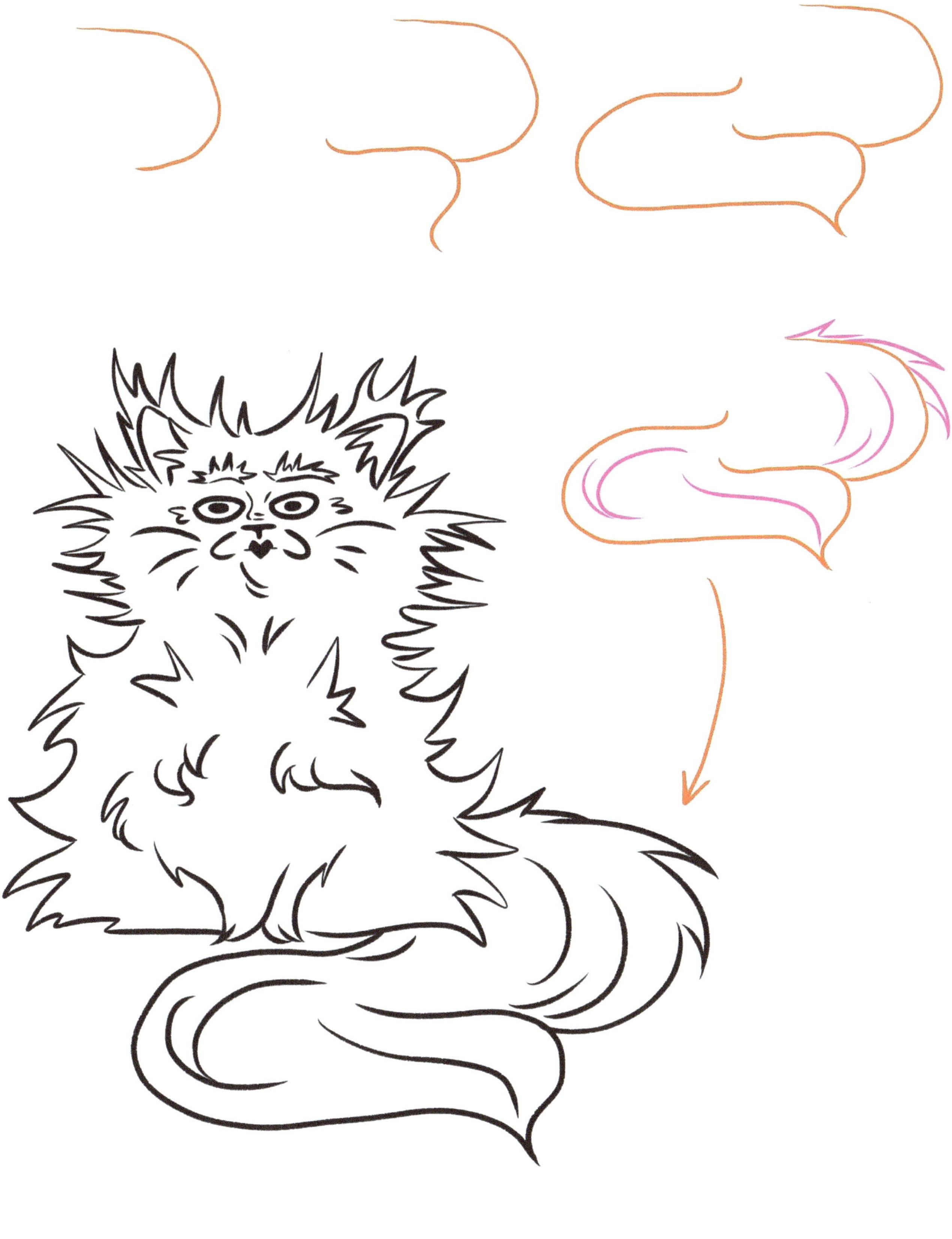

www.ingramcontent.com/pod-product-compliance
Lightning Source LLC
Chambersburg PA
CBHW050805180526
45159CB00004B/1555
* 9 7 8 1 0 7 1 3 8 0 7 5 8 *